Audrey Meadows

Love, Alice

Love, Alice

My Life as a Honeymooner

Audrey Meadows

with Joe Daley

CROWN PUBLISHERS, INC.   NEW YORK

Published by Crown Publishers, Inc., 201 East 50th Street, New York, New York 10022. Member of the Crown Publishing Group.

Random House, Inc. New York, Toronto, London, Sydney, Auckland

CROWN is a trademark of Crown Publishers, Inc.

Manufactured in the United States of America

Design by June Bennett-Tantillo

Library of Congress Cataloging-in-Publication Data
Meadows, Audrey.
Love, Alice : my life as a Honeymooner / by Audrey Meadows with Joseph A. Daley.
p.   cm.
1. Honeymooners (Television program)   2. Meadows, Audrey.
3. Gleason, Jackie, 1916–1987.   I. Daley, Joseph A.   II. Title.
PN1992.77.H623M43   1994
791.45'72—dc20
94-5870
CIP

ISBN 0-517-59881-7

10 9 8 7 6 5 4 3 2 1

First Edition

I dedicate this book to my beloved husband, Bob Six. I read somewhere, "They say in marriage a woman gives the best years of her life to a man. But in a happy marriage she gives those years to the man who made them the best."
And that was my Bob.

★ ACKNOWLEDGMENTS ★

In the course of writing this book I had occasion to relive so many memories, and had the privilege of sharing so many of them with dear friends who were a part of those wild and exciting times.

My heartfelt gratitude goes out to some of the very special people who contributed so much to my project: handsome Leonard Stern; faithful Phil Cuoco; sparkling Joan Reichman; versatile George Petrie; accomplished Andy Russell; tuneful Jerry Bresler; and wonderful Walter Stone.

Plus Bill Mark, the photographer, who at my urging made me look enough like Alice Kramden that I actually got the job.

My thanks also to the overworked Terri Navarra and Norma Salas for their encouragement, and to my editor, Peter Ginna, and the entire Crown Publishing Group for their enthusiasm and cooperation. And special thanks to my attorney, Robert B. Barnett, for his guidance and belief in this book.

All these people helped make this book possible.

Love, Alice

Alexander Graham Bell has a lot to answer for, if you ask me.

Ever since he taught us to say "Hello" into a machine, Palmer Method penmanship has gone to hell, and no one can spell anymore either. The only people who write you with any frequency don't want your heart forever. It's your wallet they're after. What did you get in the mail yesterday? Notification that you just may have won $50 million from some box number in Idaho; solicitations to cure social, human, animal, and plant illnesses; and, of course, the telephone bill.

No one writes love letters anymore, something you can stick in the edge of your mirror that memorializes times of fun and sadness, love and effort, and the trillion souvenirs of sharing an hour or a life with someone who remembers too. We've let our fingers do the walking instead of the writing, and the flow of ideas, which started with the goose quill, ended with Call Waiting.

Well, this is a love letter (with lots of postage due) to my television husband, Ralph Kramden (a.k.a. Jackie Gleason), in recollection of grand, rare, nutsy days and nights when "The Honeymooners" was America's Saturday-night ritual. We never dreamed it would still be playing in America and all over the world forty years later!

This is not a full-scale biography of Jackie. Years ago, I read two of those: one was by a reporter doing the Freud bit, rapping Jackie for being happy when the writer wanted him sad, and the other was bar stories aged to taste. So this effort is no full-scale biography, nor does it presume to plumb Jackie's psyche or ego, nor is it judgmental about how he lived his life.

My main source is myself. For years, I shared a television life with this man and enjoyed the fiction of being married to him before millions of people, so what I describe usually happened within my sight and hearing. If I wasn't on the set at the time but I heard about it, I checked with one of my buddies and credited him or her as the witness. Scattered in random fashion throughout the book are snapshots of Jackie at work and play which didn't seem to fit any particular chapter, so I feel it is okay to seed the snapshots where he might have paused for a har-de-har laugh at himself.

The life of "The Honeymooners" cast was rarely marked by order and precision, so please do not expect the cohesion of a carefully segmented work of literature to follow. When our Mr. Gleason would experience distress at scripting or stage direction or find displeasure in things unknown, he would trash a scene in midperformance and whisper that from here on out we would do it Civil War style. This meant we would follow a general into battle, observing his inspirations to complete the performance. Three guesses who the general was. Such excursions from the norm creep into this effort.

So, these remembrances of Life at the Front may lack artful linkage or fail to build sure steps to celebratory denouement and then slide down to smiles all around and gentle amens. "The Honeymooners"' pace ranged from vigorous to manic. It was exactly like putting on a Broadway play every week—a different Broadway play every week—which left little time for keeping a daily log.

All of which means the chronology of incidents may be imprecise but not the fact of their occurrence. "Consistency is the hobgoblin of small minds," as Ralph said. Waldo Emerson, not Kramden, I mean.

For those who purchased this book seeking scandalous thrills of backstage hanky-panky, lurid confessions of outrageous liaisons, all I can tell you is, we were all too tired, but we did have a lot of laughs that may make you smile too.

And if you think I'm too admiring of Jackie in this book, with not enough negative cracks, well, this is a love letter, not a report card.

I could have expressed all of the above in a preface, but I wanted someone to read it, and I've never read a preface in my life, have you?

Okay, Jackie! Got your carnation? Big opening!

Here I come. . . .

How Audrey Became Alice

O Lord, O Lord, O Lord, please throw me a lifeline—again.

Top Banana, my show, and starring Phil Silvers, of course, was winding down its Broadway run in the late summer of 1952. We were getting set to go on the road for one-week stands in theatres of capricious acoustics and temperamental lighting. I would miss my very own apartment, the brassy, breezy fun of Manhattan, the theatre and nightlife, and a couple of dependable boyfriends. All of this to be swapped for seeing the sights in Syracuse or Toledo or Des Moines, where I'd lose my voice, or my contacts, just as I did when I was on the road in *High Button Shoes*.

It had been a long climb up a slippery rope from when I had spent a year studying voice under firm Madame Gerster-Gardini to my first recital as a sixteen-year-old coloratura soprano at Carnegie Hall. Grand opera was not for me, but, seemingly, everything else in Show Business was, from operettas in New Jersey's Paper Mill Playhouse to radio musicals with Bert Lahr and Olga San Juan. Plus as the chanteuse in nightclubs from Philadelphia to Boston to Atlanta (I thought *chanteuse* meant a girl singer while to the owner it meant he could charge a minimum). My mother, a proper lady and wife of an Episcopal missionary, with fourteen years of China service, was a little concerned when I told her I had landed a job at Bill Bertolotti's in Greenwich Village, New York. Mother didn't know Bill, but she'd heard whispers about the Village.

Besides being the headline singer, I was also mistress of ceremonies for the same money. Performers starting out are always hungry, and I was no exception. Bertolotti's was famous for great Italian food, and I loved coming to work every night.

Now I was already hungry again for the sights, sounds, and smells of New York, and I hadn't even left yet. They didn't call it the Big Apple then, as I recall, or Gotham, or any of those hokey names. It was just the Big Time of Show Business—radio, records, theatre, the new television sensation! When you recall New York in the fifties, it's like thinking about some Never-Never Land. It was the headquarters of business, finance, publishing, communications, fashion, and shipping. It was bursting with people—far more than there are today. It was also a busy manufacturing center. It just absorbed into millions of jobs people from all over the nation as well as the displaced persons of World War II, who were still coming over. The place was dynamic, exciting, hectic, crazy, and altogether thrilling.

And I would have to leave it all for a Pullman upper and guided tours of the local gasworks. Having been on the road for two years (starring in *High Button Shoes*), I was not looking forward to another road company.

After returning from my first road trip, I was out of work for quite a while, getting an occasional TV show but not enough to sweeten my bank account. Out of desperation, I called a friend in the music business to ask whom he knew I could get an interview with for a job. He gave it some thought and called one day to say, "I made an appointment for you with Bill Burnham at NBC tomorrow at two." The next day I went to NBC, and when I arrived at the office, realized I had reached the top of the line.

Mr. Burnham was a big, warm teddy bear of a guy and in charge of all the major shows on the network. I sat down, and we stared at each other in silence for a beat. When he said, "What can I do for you, Miss Meadows?" I knew the interview was going to be a disaster. He didn't have a clue as to who I was or what I did. He was just being gracious to his friend.

Out of sheer nerves and an odd sense of humor, I said, "Mr. Burnham, I live in a very small apartment, and I have so much talent that when I wake up in the morning, the vibrations are so strong they hit the walls and I have to go out in the hall or the street."

I thought he would laugh and I could make an exit. But he said, "Uh huh," and waited for me to go on. Stuck with it, I said, "It doesn't really matter what I do, I just don't think it's fair to the American public that I'm not on a show." No laugh. Another "Uh huh."

I blabbed on till I'm sure he was convinced I was definitely not dealing from a full deck, and, needing safety in numbers from the woman gone prisoner to her mouth, he said, "Well, while you're here, maybe you should meet some of the boys." He buzzed, and in came top producers Ezra

Stone and Joe de Santis, whom I knew only by their track records. I chatted with them for a while, until Ezra Stone interrupted my hymn to myself by asking, "Can you play the harp?" obviously for some sketch they were casting. I said, "Gosh, Mr. Stone, I haven't played the harp in years, could you make it the violin?" I was saved from total disaster when one of them, I don't remember which, said, "Whatever she does, we must remember Miss Meadows does a mean soft shoe." Thank God, he had caught the show in Chicago, so at least one of them knew me.

When I got home and remembered what I had said, I thought to myself, "Make it the violin? I can't play the violin either!" I had played the violin as a little girl over station KDKA in Pittsburgh. I was awful.

Taking lessons later, I was screeching on the poor instrument and, out of embarrassment, said to my teacher that I had better put some more rosin on my bow. As I did, the rosin flew out of my hand and went over behind the piano. My teacher said, "It might be better if you threw the violin behind the piano." I got the message, and that was the last lesson I had.

In one of the world's great non sequiturs, Mr. Burnham asked me if I could meet with Bob and Ray on Friday. Feeling I could elude the landlord for that long, I agreed with the consummate dignity and grace I had displayed throughout the interview.

Bob Elliott and Ray Goulding were two of the sweetest and certainly most patient men ever created, I discovered, as on Friday again I was faced with not one but two quiet men. They didn't help me at all. Being born a nervous wreck and with being out of work adding to my nervousness, I went into my nonstop spiel, babbling along, cascades of words, words, words.

Just before their collapse under fire, Bob hesitatingly raised a hand. I paused to inhale. "Do you think you could start on Monday?" he asked.

"What will I do?"

Bob: "You'll play a character called Linda Lovely—and it will be very easy for you."

"Oh, how is that?"

Bob: "Well, Linda Lovely never speaks."

I've always thought he made that up just at that moment. That was their kind of humor. Linda Lovely lived in a small but pretentious house on the side of a hill with her Uncle Eugene, and she was one of my favorite characters. Later, when they found I really wasn't too very, very strange, I became part of the improvisational comedy, which demanded every skill you could bring into play.

Masters of satire and irony, Bob and Ray were subtle gamesters in a sport in which, if you had to ask the rules, you weren't up to the competition. Both were former highly successful Boston radio announcers rather than Show Biz veterans. They established a kind of spurious dignity for their fantasy characters, whose jobs or goals or habits might be a trifle awry, yet who spoke coherently from the center of a fuzzy world.

Starting in the fall of 1951, the two years I played with the team were a joy. We were on five nights a week from 7:15 to 7:30. I was a seasoned actress before I joined them, but their inspirational style was so rich and varied that you had to be on your toes and allow yourself to be totally free to join in their improvisations. Bob and Ray knew each other so well that they could create characters as they went along. Rather than a formal script, we started with a premise or general outline and took it from there.

You had to dance through the minefield of their banter

and feel when it was right to zing a couple of your own wildies. In effect, you were expected to direct yourself within the team concept. They were both brilliant and satirized everything on TV—soap operas, interviews, et cetera—and they received tons of fan mail, more than many of the big shows on NBC at that time.

Such experience has more in common with catch-as-catch-can wrestling than with the Thea-tah, but it demanded instant responses and the certainty that you could handle any surprise. When we got a sponsor, Old Gold cigarettes, the boys had to write scripts to submit, but we never followed them. They were just something to turn in. Somehow no one seemed to notice we weren't doing anything they had written.

The show had been "sustaining"—meaning without a sponsor—up until then. I assume sponsors were a little gun-shy about the many satires we did on products. We had a fictitious Overstocked Surplus Warehouse sketch. On one show we offered surplus football sweaters with a big *O* for people who were named O'Reilly, O'Toole, Olshevsky, and so on, and we said they could be had for a song.

Several weeks later, NBC came to Bob and Ray and said, "What shall we do with all this sheet music?"

Bob said, "What sheet music?"

"The hundreds of letters that have come in to buy the *O* sweaters."

Bob sighed. "Where did we go wrong? They're starting to believe us."

Naturally, I had no idea that this marine boot training I was undergoing was fashioning me for combat at *The Honeymooners'* cannon's mouth.

At 7:30 P.M. each day, that would be me whirling out of 30 Rockefeller Plaza, still in TV makeup, sprinting down

Love, Alice

Fiftieth Street to the Winter Garden Theatre on Broadway and *Top Banana,* my second job. Curtain at 8:40, and I had just enough time to scrub off TV makeup, apply stage cosmetics, and get into costume for Act I (won't someone give me a bite of their sandwich? Puh-leeze!). The show was peppy, funny, had bouncy tunes by Johnny Mercer and a great star, Phil Silvers, who later, as Sergeant Bilko, would become more famous than he ever had been in movies or on the stage.

Television had struggled to life in the late forties but skyrocketed in the borning fifties. It had completely buried network radio and was leaving Hollywood wounded and wailing. And New York was home to all the big shows—*The Ed Sullivan Show, Studio One, Your Show of Shows,* Arthur Godfrey's shows, *Robert Montgomery Presents, Omnibus, Person to Person, Today, The Tonight Show, Home. . . .* Movies had only gone to California because they could film outdoors all year there. But television looked as if it had found its home right in Manhattan, and no real New Yorkers wanted to leave, as they said, until, like the elephants, they got old and went to Miami Beach to die.

New York has changed enormously over the years (and so have all our other cities), but all those young people who look at the old black and white movies in which New York starred as much as the actors have got to understand that it really was a wonder world then. Better than spectacular.

It was a classy town all the way and every way—the best jazz, the finest nightclubs (yes, Virginia, there really were nightclubs, not eating places with Muzak). Its syndicated columnists from Walter Winchell to Dorothy Kilgallen told the nation, and the world, what was happening in Manhattan, and the whole globe came to know whatever the local street addresses meant—Fifth Avenue, Broadway, Forty-second Street, Wall Street, Times Square, Madison Avenue. . . .

The place was a tonic, a trip, exhilarating—yes, glamorous!

In great part, this was due to New Yorkers themselves. It was as if most of them were reading for parts in a show themselves. You must remember that, at this time, there was remarkably little street crime in such a vast and heavily populated area. *Mugging* was a word unfamiliar to most of the citizens. It wasn't at all unusual for a guy to see his date home on the East Side and cut through Central Park at 2:00 A.M. to his home on the West Side without any hesitation. The carnage of the drug scene was unknown and unsuspected.

The subway was the fastest and simplest way to get from here to there, whether you were a stockbroker or a shoeshine boy (no one worried about rider safety). All New York kids went to P.S. something, and the local education was demanding and rewarding. Of course, there were no cops in the halls to enforce discipline. The blue uniforms of parochial school kids were seen all over the city, but posh private schools were so rare as to be suspect.

New York had been called an ethnic melting pot, but it wasn't in the fifties, and I doubt if it had ever been. There were clearly delineated neighborhoods of Italians, Germans, Irish, Chinese, Blacks, Poles, and Jews, even Visigoths or Aztecs, for all I know. The civil works experts probably had decided to tear down acres of old neighborhood blocks in the fifties to create the soulless fortresses of public housing, since ex-GI's and their families were moving to Levittown and South Orange so their kids could grow up looking at a tree. Naturally, this destruction for construction's sake forever changed the face and the heart and the spirit of New York too.

I lived and worked in midtown Manhattan (roughly Forty-second to Fifty-ninth streets), and I often wondered why I had an agent and a manager. Walking down Seventh or Broadway or Sixth (no one ever called it Avenue of the Americas), I would meet more pals and get more job offers than if I had stayed on the phone doing nothing but calling producers. Every part of the city was compartmentalized to the people who worked in it, which always confused out-of-towners. Someone from the Bronx would be hopelessly lost if he crossed the Brooklyn Bridge, and Queens was a mystery to people who lived in Brooklyn, but all were acquainted with Manhattan. People from the other four boroughs, whether going to the Metropolitan Opera or Madison Square Garden, said they were "going to the City."

While New York was, and is, composed of hundreds of nationalities, there was in the fifties no profound yearning for a particular homeland. (Even the Irish spirit on St. Patrick's Day, I have been assured by March 17 marchers, is confined to singing old songs and raising friendly jars rather than any passion to return). Too many New Yorkers, then, were first-generation Americans with clear recollections of the autocratic justice, frozen caste systems, and enforced social barriers which curbed education and advancement in the Old Country. New Yorkers had become superpatriots of America and were not wistful about having made the change from abroad.

A few final words about the people of New York. They have gotten a bad rap all over the country as being a stereotype—patronizing, rude, and loud. The French feel the same about people from Paris, the English about those London toffs, the Russians about the high-steppers from Moscow. My family has been part of New York since Fourteenth Street was the country, and I'm saying, "Ain't so."

To live in New York is a test of valor and patience. In winter, it is colder than Iceland. In summer the humidity, on top of the heat, will fry your brain and should produce mayhem in the streets, except it's too hot to fight! Millions of people jammed together in confined areas have produced a community wherein people live elbow-to-elbow rather than arm-in-arm. Also, the city has too many people to ever be really clean, and its record for morality in civic government is underwhelming. You would think living under these conditions would be intolerable. Wrong.

Ask New Yorkers George Burns, Mel Brooks, Woody Allen, Neil Simon, and recall all of the Marx Brothers. New Yorkers are funny, flippant, and feisty. It's the only way to live there. You have to be part of Show Business. You can't just watch. Everyone in New York is a part-time comic actor, to ignore the realities of Life in the Big City.

And I was being forced into exile with a two-suiter, a makeup box, and my second-best raincoat for the clickety-clack music of the New York Central Railroad and some aging hotel in somebody's theatre district (a short walk to a double feature). Shuffle off to Elba. . . .

"Audrey," called my manager, Val Irving, from my apartment door, shattering reveries, "look who I brought to see you!"

Handsome and smiling Val entered with a guy who was short, bald, and worried. He was "Bullets" Durgom, manager of Jackie Gleason, the comic who'd scored an improbable success the previous season on the tiny DuMont network (now WABC-TV in New York) with a breezy variety show called *Cavalcade of Stars*. It was peopled by a Gleason gallery of characters, ranging from Joe the Bartender to The

Poor Soul and Reggie Van Gleason III and an ensemble spot with Art Carney and Pert Kelton titled, for no good reason, "The Honeymooners"—skits about the raucous dueling of a Brooklyn bus driver and his wife. Gleason's local show had pushed, and even topped, the high-budget network spots opposite him, and he had been scheduled for a full hour on Saturday night by CBS.

"I ran into Bullets on the way over to see you, Audrey," Val was saying. "The Gleason show has a big problem. Pert Kelton had a heart attack and won't be able to play the wife's role in 'The Honeymooners.' They've been searching for a replacement, but everyone is contracted for something else or not right for one reason or another. You know just about every actress in New York, so I asked him to come along to see if you knew someone who might be just right for the role that he hadn't thought of."

Help your girlfriend and she'll help you (or she better!) is an unwritten motto of actresses. It's the kind of old boy networking which has become the golden secret of executive recruitment of big business today.

I must have named a full registry of actresses (plus girls who would learn to be a Rockette overnight to get a job). It almost made me forget about my own upcoming exile to the provinces. Almost.

After two hours, Bullets's dark Lebanese features had become etched in dread as each of my candidates appeared to be too old, too young, too pregnant, in Hollywood, wanted too much money, or was a lush. And they had already interviewed everyone I mentioned.

"I've got it!" I exclaimed in a tone used for announcing the discovery of radium. "The perfect girl, oh, you're so dumb, she'll be fabulous."

Both men said, "Who? Who?"

I said, "Me."

Silence.

Bullets: "Come on, Audrey, be serious."

I said, "I am serious. You said he's seen everyone, so why not make an appointment for me?"

So the next afternoon with Val, I went to meet Jackie Gleason at his office, with Bullets blending into the wallpaper following an unnecessary introduction. Actually, I'd met Jackie months before when Eddie Hanley, who was in *Top Banana* with me, had taken me to The Embers after the show to hear Joe Bushkin, the famous piano player. Jackie Gleason came to our table because he knew Eddie and had a drink with us. Wherever there was good music, you could find Jackie, I was to learn.

Jackie was being interviewed and photographed by *Life* magazine when I arrived, so it was certainly an awkward time to visit, but he was cordial and hospitable, breaking away from the magazine group to meet with me. Here are some first impressions of him on the edge of his Big Time debut.

Naturally handsome, he was stylishly barbered and groomed, dressed comfortably and well. This was no overweight slob. He had a pleasantly modulated and unhurried voice, so unlike the husky rasp or side-of-the-mouth slur he used in character. Unlike many actors and most comedians, he was not on when he was offstage. He didn't focus attention on himself but chatted broadly about a range of subjects using a varied vocabulary and often precise words.

I would learn later that he also never used coarse language when women were present. Many comics would come to visit Jackie on Saturdays in his dressing room, and if four-letter words started to fly around when Joyce Randolph, who portrayed Trixie Norton in "The Honeymooners," and I were present, Jackie would say, "Watch it, the girls are here!" Like many men of his time and upbringing, he divided women between ladies and hookers and schooled his manners to his perception of the female he was addressing.

As a professional comic, he was known as a great reaction player, whose expressive eyes and mobile face were ideal for television close-ups. ("The test of a real comedian is whether you laugh at him before he opens his mouth," critic George Jean Nathan had said. He had Gleason right.) Because he was big, Jackie featured physical comedy too—lots of flapping limb movements, trips and sprawls, and pratfalls. But even at his heaviest (and that was very heavy), his physical stunts were so smooth and coordinated that they amazed fellow performers. Despite his size, he was agile enough to make a perilous fall funny for the crowd and graceful to appreciative actors.

I was the one who, more or less, ended the meeting, well aware that the *Life* crew was getting restless, and while Gleason was being gracious, no performer wants to irritate the press. I exited to my own cue, and he asked Val and Bullets to stay.

I waited outside for Val by the elevators, and when he appeared, he had the look of a friend about to tell you that your dog has died.

"What did he say, Val?"

"He said, 'Why don't you two guys take the needles out of your heads? She's all wrong—she's too young and too pretty! I'll give you she's charming, witty, neat, and smart—everything that Alice Kramden definitely is not.'"

Now I had asked for this interview, more or less, as a lark, but when I realized he'd turned me down, I was very disappointed. I would not have minded a producer saying that, but a man of Jackie's talent should have known I could play the part.

Val walked me back to my apartment, and suddenly an idea came to me. I said, "Val, can you get a photographer to come to my apartment first thing in the morning to photograph me with no makeup? Better get Bill Mark, because he'll have to develop and print the shots by the afternoon so we can get them up to Jackie the same day. They're going to have to make up their minds pretty quickly, because they only have a little over two weeks before he goes on the air, so we need to work fast. I won't get out of bed till you ring the bell, and we'll get some pictures of me taken looking like his idea of Alice."

Getting Val out of the apartment while ignoring his objections, I began to plot my wardrobe for the character of Alice. I went through my closet looking for an old blouse, a skirt and apron, a hair net, curlers, and some combs to pull my hair up and make it scraggly looking. I figured I was ready for the morning. Of course, this was pretty dreamy stuff, considering the boss had just told me politely, You're a peach, kid. Good luck and good traveling.

Everyone who knows me is aware that not even my reflexes to pain wake up when the alarm goes off. Came the dawn or a reasonable facsimile, and photographer Bill Mark leaned on the bell. I successfully reached the front door without opening my eyes, lit a cigarette while squinting my right eye cautiously, since you get your nose seared if you don't carefully watch your wavering fingers push fire at you, and started to make coffee as the lens of the Speed Graphic whirred noisily for such an early hour.

As phases of consciousness began to stir, I started to do

adventurous things like wash a cup or run the carpet sweeper over my bare foot or attempt to apply lipstick while smoking, which may well become an Olympic event. My mother, who was there, was alarmed by what I was doing. She kept saying, "Oh, darling, fix your hair, and you're making terrible faces." Bill was surprised too—he thought he had come to take glamour pictures of me, but soon he was amused and got into the act. I told him these pictures had to get me a job.

I had revved up to a sickly smile and was offering to make him a sandwich by a couple of hours later, when he had shot himself out of film and departed. I collapsed into deep sloth while Bill processed the assembled photos of Meadows aka Alice Kramden and Val got a set over to Bullets by 4:00, after running by the apartment to show them to me.

I looked dreadful.

It was perfect!

No makeup, hair a mess, that ruined blouse hiding a hint of bargain basement skirt. Without a cosmetician and wardrobe mistress, I thought I'd done okay. Now, we'd just see. . . .

We instructed Bullets under no condition to identify the actress.

Bullets told us what happened when he showed the photos to Jackie, identifying the subject just as a "good actress who really wants the part." Jackie glowed as he studied each sorry pose, ending with a shout. "That's our Alice! Who is she? Where is she? Can we get her?"

Bullets said, "That's the girl who was here yesterday, Audrey Meadows, and she arranged the photo shoot to show she could look the part as well as play it." Jackie cheered both the imagination and the stunt. He said,

"Any dame with a sense of humor like that deserves the job!"

He was also more than a little relieved. "The Honeymooners" had become one of the hit segments on *Cavalcade of Stars*, and he had to have a new Alice by the opening show. "Hire her" was his simple order to Bullets Durgom.

As a man of legendary thrift with Gleason's budget, Bullets muted Jackie's more admiring adjectives when he reported them to Val and me back at my apartment. In the mind of Bullets, who had been next to weeping about his desperate need to find a talented performer for Alice Kramden and fast, the focus of our discussion had now shifted to fee for services, and he became reserved and reverential when money was spoken of aloud, especially when it was vaguely under his supervision. It became more than personal. Sacred would come close.

Short and sly, Bullets was the most agile dancer outside the Bolshoi when dollars were discussed. My manager, Val, was also adept at all the contractual steps and dips, not to mention the grips and holds of Greco-Roman wrestling, but somehow, when the deal was done, I was hired to work every other week and signed a separate contract for each show.

In a risky business, the risk became all mine. I had bailed out of a surefire, long-running Broadway show to join a one-person-missing comedy quartet which had not yet played to a network audience. If we faltered, CBS surely had ten movies in the can to cover. And, with no annual contract, I would be at liberty to read for the ingenue's fruitcake sister or do crowd noises on radio.

This was not part of my master plan.

So I vowed that I would play the socks off Alice Kramden and prayed that the show would be a blockbuster hit, because the alternative was most depressing.

Being the daughter of missionary parents in China, I was raised to be an optimist, and my mother took on the continent of Asia all by herself. So I guessed I could stand up to Jackie Gleason. After all, Asia is bigger. Isn't it?

★ SNAPSHOT ★

When I took the job, I made it very clear to all concerned that I would be happy to play the role until Pert Kelton recovered. I did not want to get a job on someone's hard luck. I was told emphatically that if I started with them I would stay with them.

It was several years later that I discovered the real reason why Pert Kelton did not make the move from *Cavalcade of Stars* to the big show at CBS.

We were doing "The Adoption" script, and an actress was hired to do the baby cries offstage. I was asked to let her share my dressing room. Chatting with her, I discovered that she was a good friend of Pert Kelton.

"How is Miss Kelton, is she getting better?" I inquired.

"She's just fine, there's nothing wrong with her" came the reply.

"I thought she had a very serious heart attack and couldn't work."

I was stunned when she said, "She can't work because she was blacklisted." This was the fifties and the infamous days of the witch hunt which ruined many careers.

Chalk one up for Jackie. He was not about to hurt Pert Kelton further by spreading the story. It was kinder to say she was ill.

★ SNAPSHOT ★

A story Jackie delighted in telling about himself occurred long before he was touched with any kind of fame or even much steady work. As a young man in the business, he was an emcee-comic in intimate bistros, which required a good punch, along with a good punch line, to overcome the imbibing hecklers.

On a brief holiday, he booked a room in a hotel on the Jersey shore for a little surf bathing. (As difficult as it is to believe, our Jackie had been lithe enough, then, to be a trick diver in what passed as minor aquacades. We told him he would certainly make a big splash now. He was not amused.)

Anyway, his habit of overtipping everyone who didn't have his hands in his pockets ran wild at this little hotel. Too wild. The generous guest discovered in the privacy of his room that he had tipped himself into penury. He called a friend who had a car to meet him and proceeded to dress in layers of all his clothes, rolling up the pant legs and wrapping himself in a huge robe. Descending to the lobby, he waved gaily to the desk, sang out that he was off for a bracing dip in the Atlantic, and waddled off to find his friend and flee while clothed in a respectable man's haberdashery.

Sometime later (a year? two?), when his cash was marginally ahead of his markers, Jackie went back to the shore hotel he'd beaten out of the rent, carrying remorse and money.

"Hi," he saluted blithely to the owner at the front desk, who gazed at him with startled eyes. "I brought you the money I owe you."

"Oh, my God!" the hotel man yelled. "We thought you had drowned!"

Jackie considered his resurrection the world's best return performance.

How Alice Became Audrey

Before I would be in any position to accept the role of Alice, I would have to plead my case to Phil Silvers, star and boss of *Top Banana*. Phil was a sweetheart of a guy, but I had to ask him to let me out of my contract without the customary full two weeks' notice, and he would have to recast my role with the show headed for the road. A sweetheart he was, but I was asking him to become Santa Claus.

I took Bill Mark's pictures to the Winter Garden Theatre to show Phil that night. Honesty being the best policy, or, in this case, the only one, I told him my sad or happy story, depending on your point of view. To prove to him how much I wanted the part, I showed him the candid prints. I groaned about how dreadful they made me look to fill in dead air as Phil meticulously examined each photo slowly and without comment and my blood pressure wandered into infinity. If he, as he had the perfect right to do, held me to my contract, it would be "Hello, Harrisburg, and Good-bye, 'Honeymooners.' " I may have started out for the Alice part on little more than a whim, but it had become a fervent dream over the last couple of days.

Phil laid the last Audrey-as-dowdy-Alice photo down and said blandly, "I don't know what you're complaining about. You should look so good." He started to look a lot like Santa right there.

I began to tell him how sorry I was to leave him short, but he interrupted with "That's my problem, and I'll handle it. It's not your problem anymore, Aud." I either got or gave a big smackeroo of a kiss for luck and for friendship and for old times and new laughs. Phil Silvers, one of the best.

While Jackie was naturally the star of *The Jackie Gleason Show,* an equal top banana (the old burlesque term for the lead comic) was Art Carney. I guess if you want to be a purist about such things, he would be second banana if the star chose to be the top of the bunch. Art was, and is, one of the most endearing men I have ever met—a witty and de-lightful companion who went out of his way to help each new actor find his niche in the often bewildering world of *The Jackie Gleason Show.* He also was the owner-operator of one of the most recognizable characters in American TV—Ed Norton, sewer worker extraordinaire!

Actually, Art had put Norton together over the years in radio parts and on *The Morey Amsterdam Show,* styling voice and mannerisms. When Gleason writers Arnie Rosen and Coleman Jacoby introduced him to Jackie, Art had found his comedic partner for life, starting with the *Caval-cade* show on DuMont. The writers could script the show, but the Irish leprechauns inhabiting Kramden and Norton always added bits of inspired banter or business, which transformed giggles into belly laughs.

Art had come to Jackie after developing a great character known as Newton the Waiter. This was on *The Morey Amsterdam Show* at DuMont. Morey told me Art was a one-man band. He could sing, dance, play the piano, and become any character as if it were written just for him.

Jackie had borrowed Art from Morey for a part on *Cavalcade of Stars,* and it was instant comic synergy between them. Jackie knew he had found a fantastic one-two punch for his show, and he asked Morey if Art could please stay with him.

But Art had a problem similar to mine. He had almost two years left to go on his contract with Morey. Proving that there was more than one lovable boss in Show Business, Morey tore up Art's contract and wished him success with Gleason. Art, stunned, said, "No one else in show business would do this!"

Morey always says, "I'm the happiest man I know."

And we all know why.

No one out front, of course, realized that Art personally was one of the most shy people you'd ever meet, very humble, no towering ego, no relation at all to the zany extrovert whom he called the Senior Superintendent of Subterranean Sanitation.

I myself admit to an early extreme shyness, which in some ways has never really left me completely. As a child, I was a bit of a tomboy. I loved to play cops and robbers with my brothers, until one day while chasing them I fell through a skylight, seriously slashing my left leg, and was rushed to the hospital. My leg was so twisted and full of glass that the doctor wanted to amputate at the knee, but my mother's tears and prayers and hours of begging him to save the leg won out. Two operations followed. However, the doctor told my mother that I would never run again and probably not even walk well.

The leg healed, but my pain over the unsightly scars didn't. This only compounded my shyness. Playing on the beach I had to wear a white stocking, which naturally caused all the other kids to ask, "What's the matter with your leg?" Or worse, just to point at me and laugh. It's an overdone cliché, but children can be so cruel.

Of course, in time the scars on my leg paled and faded, but not those in my mind. I was fine, but I had created and nurtured a handicap which was invisible except to me, over-looking entirely the miracle that the accident had not changed the shape of my leg. When I no longer needed to wear the stocking, the scars were that awful purplish red. For years when in a room with strangers it was second nature for me to sit with that leg folded under me.

Every day I thank my mother for her wisdom in not telling me what the doctor had said. By the time I was in boarding school, I was the fastest runner on the field hockey team. It was my mother's belief (and mine) to resist any negative thinking. If I had been told that I could not run, perhaps I never would have. Or danced. And to this day, when shyness sometimes hits me, I'll ask myself, Now where did that come from?

I got to know Art quite well because he was virtually the only member of the cast I met during "The Case of the Missing Rehearsals." I was called each day for a rehearsal at 11:00 A.M. at the Park Sheraton Hotel, where the receptionist would usher me into the living room. I'd say hello to Art, and we'd sit for a while, and then Jackie's secretary, Lee Reynolds, would appear and say, "Oh, my goodness, didn't anyone tell you? Jackie had to go to a meeting. Come to-morrow at the same time."

Tomorrow the story was "So sorry, Jackie has a dentist's appointment. Come tomorrow."

I would stammer, "I can't—I have a matinee."

Lee: "Oh, that's right, you're still in the show."

Another day, surprise, surprise, Jackie was there and there were scripts on the coffee table! I was ecstatic because he had not yet heard me read for the part. Sadly, there was a photographer there. We had publicity pictures taken holding the scripts, and then Jackie was off again and I was given a call for the following day.

The second week was a repetition of the first, and I was becoming more and more nervous. They had all worked together before; I was the only new kid on the block. By Friday, I was sure Jackie would have to be there as I was now becoming an apprentice psychopath.

By this time, I knew every inch of that living room, how many steps it took to walk to the couch, and the size of the big new TV set of which Jackie was so proud. In the fifties the status symbol was the enormous wooden cabinet the TV was set in, with big speakers on either side. It took up half of one wall.

Art had confided to me that Jackie didn't like to rehearse much. Understatement of the year! I turned to Art and said, "I know where he is. He's not at the doctor's or a dentist— he's at Toots Shor's celebrating his big new contract. Why don't we go there for lunch? He's always there for lunch, and he won't miss a day like today."

Art: "We can't go there."

Me: "Why not? It's a public place."

Art took a lot of persuading, but finally he acquiesced. I said, "I know where he'll be sitting, the first table on the left, so don't look over there when we walk in. We'll pretend we don't care that there was no rehearsal."

I had to practically drag Art in, but we sat down and

ordered lunch. Sure enough, Jackie was there with the two Jacks, Hurdle and Philbin, our producers, and assorted brass celebrating.

Jack Hurdle came over, very embarrassed and apologetic, and I said very nonchalantly, "Oh, that's okay. But if we're going to sit there, the least you could do is make sure the TV set is working."

Hurdle yelped frantically, "It's not working?"

Me: "No, it's not. Art took the back off and tried to fix it, but he couldn't."

Jack said, "Gee, thanks," and rushed off to a phone booth to find the board-certified expert on television repair who would later present Hurdle with a staggering bill for services rendered to repair a set which was never broken. We had never turned it on: we didn't dare. Revenge is sweet when it's secret.

The big day! Saturday, and my call was for 1:00 P.M., so I thought, At least we'll have a few hours to go over it. It's only one sketch, not the whole hour. We worked in Studio 50 on Fifty-third Street and Broadway. *The Ed Sullivan Show* came from there, and Arthur Godfrey's show, and many others.* It is a wonderful theatre and just the right size for comedy. We would walk in the stage door and out onto the stage and down some little steps into the audience, where we all gathered. Jackie and June Taylor were rehearsing the June Taylor Dancers in their opening number. The atmosphere was pulsing with that indefinable electricity you feel with the musicians tuning up and stage-

* It has since been renamed The Ed Sullivan Theatre and was recently remodeled for David Letterman.

hands moving flats, cameras checking positions, wardrobe people double-checking costumes. It's a mighty high. Enough to make you want to laugh out loud or throw up, and if it doesn't stir your senses, go back to selling hot dogs or mutual funds.

The next one up after the dancers was our guest star, singer Eileen Barton. She had a good full rehearsal as I watched the hands on the big clock on the wall move inexorably on. Jackie was doing sketches of his other characters as well as "The Honeymooners," so finally our set was moved into place. The curtains were closed, and our announcer, Jack Lescoulie, made the introduction. We went up onstage and ran through the sketch once in our own clothes, and without props. Then it was back sitting in the audience as rehearsals continued. That clock was becoming my enemy as it closed on 5:00. Finally, I turned to Art and said, "When do we do the blocking?" He said, "You just did it." I said, "Well, when do we do a run-through?" He said, "You just did it." Terrified to hear his next answer, I still braved it and asked, "When is dress rehearsal?" Yes, he did—he said, "You just did it!"

I sat in numbed silence as big tears rolled down my cheeks. Val, my wonderful manager, became very undone and said, "Don't cry, don't cry. Your eyes will swell up and be all red and you'll look awful." He understood what I was feeling because he'd been a performer himself. I had just left a Broadway show, for which you rehearse until you drop, and now I was going to go before the whole population of the United States and wing it!

Six o'clock and rehearsal was over, so I took my red eyes to my dressing room and proceeded to learn all of Jackie's and Art's lines. I knew my own. This was a habit I had picked up doing summer stock in case someone "went up" (forgot his or her next line). It was my security blanket, and it has served me well. If we were all going to go out there cold, at least I was going to be alert enough to defend myself. I don't know whether I knew then Spencer Tracy's advice on acting, "Know your lines and try not to bump into the furniture," but it seemed appropriate. Tense but prepared, I stood backstage with Jackie just before the opening of our "Honeymooners" segment, with butterflies doing barrel rolls in my stomach.

"Good luck, Miss Meadows," Jackie said, a trifle formally, possibly aware that his stage wife was less than cheerful about events to date. By then my nervousness had been transformed into a restrained fury. I regret my unprofessionalism, but I just had to sink a fang into this big, bad tyrant who would become my great friend.

"Good luck to you, Mr. Gleason," I sang. "You know, you are such a fabulous talent and you have such a gorgeous voice. I think I'm just going to go out there and listen to your beautiful voice." Jackie's smile froze on his face as he realized something was a bit awry.

"You mean you're going to throw me some bum lines?" asked the world's greatest bus driver.

"You don't understand. I'm not going to throw you any lines," I said semisweetly.

Jack Lescoulie gave the introduction to "The Honeymooners," the curtain opened, and we were on! Oddly enough, butterflies disappear as soon as you start, replaced by calm control as your concentration takes over and you become the character. Of course, when the red light on the camera blinked on and the audience out front came alive to the harried pace of the Kramdens' living room–kitchen, wherein Ralph's dynamic ideas required him to stride through people and chairs, I began to realize how a rehearsal might have set the rest of us up for a series of surprise collisions. The set was purposefully spartan and small (best for comedy) and seeking to copy Brooklyn's Chauncey Street in the Old Days. Jackie was the original man in motion, with pinwheeling arms and twisting head perpetually seeking more space. His solution, as he paced, was to straight-arm me across the chest to make room to pass. With Art, he would deliver a jab with his elbow, causing Art to do one of his funny falls that never reached the ground. Art's body always seemed to be made of Jell-O—no bones.

Frank Satenstein, our director, had no idea where Jackie was going to go, of course, any more than we did. We never had floor marks (positions you are supposed to hit for the camera). Jackie was just captured by the spirit of his momentary idea and moved with it. He was living the role, and the audience knew that and was living it with him.

Since Jackie and Art were both so physical in their characters, I decided to keep Alice very still in contrast. Unless the script had me fussing in the sink or icebox, I decided to keep Alice out of the traffic by taking up my station by the table, stage center, on the premise that Jackie would have to pass me coming and going in his parades, and he'd know where to find me, and so would the camera, if he was supposed to be talking to me. It worked.

Another thing I learned on or about that first night was the reason that Jackie delayed rehearsals until they would somehow go away. It wasn't that he was capricious or lazy or unprofessional. It was his firm feeling that repetition of comedic situations or lines injured the delivery by dulling the reception.

You could rehearse a skit before the crew and have everyone rolling on the floor with the material. This is food and drink for a comic actor. It's a lot of the reason he's up there in the first place. Yet the fourth or fifth time you do the same lines before the same crew, the party turns into a wake. And, actors being actors, the comic convinces himself he's laying a hydrogen bomb. He asks the pizza delivery kid to help him pep up the script and, after he has remade it into rotten-rotten, opens his mouth and goes down in flames when it was great in the first place.

Naturally, the forces of nature conspired to sabotage me on my "Honeymooners" debut because we hadn't rehearsed with the props. In the script, Alice had prepared husband Ralph a steak for dinner. Reaching for the prop, I was surprised to find it was a piece of wood painted to look like a steak. As I placed it before him, Ralph's line in the script was "You're not going to feed me a frozen steak again, Alice, are you?" He seized the prop steak and pounded so hard on the table with it that it proceeded to break in half. Half the phony steak flew over the top of the scenery and into the Great Beyond. The audience howled! So I said, "No, you're not getting a frozen steak. You're getting half a frozen steak!"

Back to the script, I moved to the bedroom door to make my exit, turned the knob, and . . . nothing happened. I kept shaking the knob to no avail, so I turned to Jackie and said, "And how many times have I told you to fix this door?" with which it opened. I made my exit, went up to my dressing room, changed my clothes, ran out of the theatre without waiting for the show to be over, grabbed a cab, and cried all the way home.

Being a confirmed Pollyanna, I finally decided that better days were coming.

They were and they did.

The very next morning Jackie called, obviously aware

that I had been edgy the night before. My remarks to him prior to the sketch, and my speedy getaway after it, told him I was unhappy. He declared that the only way to feel better about things was to have a party. "So I'm throwing a party for you today," said he.

I wavered in acceptance, as does anyone who thinks she should be mad rather than glad for no logical reason. But Jackie wouldn't give up, and he finally charmed me into accepting.

I arrived with Pierrot, my French poodle, and had a great time. At one point, Jackie said, "Boy, you were certainly upset last night." So I said, "Listen, Jackie, if I'm going to continue to work for you, I will call the rehearsals. And we will leave a space for you to stand, so on Saturday when you arrive to rehearse, wherever you see a space, a big space, that is for you!" He loved it.

I was to find that Jackie couldn't stand for anyone whom he liked to be angry with him. He would go to unusual ends to placate a person he considered a friend. And that day I learned that Jackie Gleason was a man of infinite charm. Smart, alert, amiable, he was a good listener as well as an interesting talker on a variety of themes, not just Show Business.

He never demanded attention but was the spark of any gathering. A good mimic, he could imagine outrageous pseudoevents for characters, as we all know. Rarely did he tell jokes, but he acted out situations using those expressive eyes and animated features to create inspired lunacy. Jackie was Jackie—the world's merry man, having a marvelous time and taking you along for the ride.

You couldn't be sulky around a man who made you laugh until the tears started. At least, I couldn't. We became friends that night and stayed that way all through the years.

I learned that one of Manhattan's most prominent Broadway beat columnists had heard me interviewed on the popular Barry Gray radio show after I was announced as the new Alice. Since Barry was a New York–style liberal's liberal and the columnist would have been thought radical in the cabinet of Calvin Coolidge, the writer had the false courage of his byline, if little else. He called Jackie to say that if Audrey Meadows was in the cast of "The Honeymooners," he would have to give it a bad review. I don't know what Jackie told him, but Bullets informed me that he would have none of it. If the Broadway Blacklister gave us a bad review, he joined a legion of himself. Score one for Jackie. Make that two. He did a nice thing and a right thing, and he didn't take bows for it.

Rehearsals were a Saturday-only affair as the weeks went on and "The Honeymooners" began getting more and more of the airtime. Jackie still adhered to his less-is-better idea of comedy rehearsals, so Art and I would take any new supporting players upstairs to our dressing rooms and continue to rehearse there. Occasionally one would say, "But I was standing there," and we'd say, "That's okay. But tonight Jackie may be in that spot." I'd say, "You just give way like you would at a party, or in your own house. Just be natural." This was not quite like walking the junior high through the class pageant.

Most of the actors were Broadway veterans, some with Hollywood time but most very new to television. As character actors, they had matured through years of training and onstage performances, which require specific discipline to the interpretation of the director. They were adaptable, responsive, and reliable up to the point when they found

Art and myself taking them to our dressing rooms to instruct them in Jackie's crossovers and exits and entrances, without, of course, Jackie. They would insist, "But I was standing there at rehearsal." I would say, "Never mind, you won't be there if he walks through you, so just move or die." Abruptly, a performer with twenty years of program credits started to become as skittish as a teenager on his first chorus cattle call.

Art and I sold our guests snake oil in large amounts, reassuring these actors that all would be marvelous on the air, and it was. But pros rarely missed a cue or muffed a line, and many stayed with "The Honeymooners" for years in one guise or another.

Some still displayed jitters on show night, and it wasn't until many years later that Art told me Jackie referred to them as "twitchers." We finally ended up with a list of what Jack Hurdle called Gleason actors, the ones with nerves of steel. They all played many characters, whatever the script called for. George Petrie, Frank Marth, Cliff Hall, Eddie Hanley, Sammy Birch, and Zamah Cunningham were practically regulars.

By the way, Jackie never denigrated or patronized, or even was testy to, an actor who had any problem with his role. Not because he was a saint but because he was an actor. And he never fired anyone either.

I enter this comment now because I have heard people who were never on *The Jackie Gleason Show* at that time say that he was tyrannical and ruled with a will of iron. Not so. Not then. Never. Never. Never. He ran the whole operation, but he never did it at the top of his voice. He never went out of his way to embarrass or humiliate a player, dancer, or crew member. He was Jackie to everybody, and he most certainly wanted to be liked, not feared.

However, when something wasn't working, he would catch the writer's eyes with a skull take. "Skull" is an old expression, probably from burlesque. It's rolling your eyes to heaven and expressing anguish. The writers had names for these various takes. If there was macaroni in the scene, it became known as the macaroni take.

While "The Honeymooners" was gaining the top spot in the gallery of Gleason sketches—Joe the Bartender, The Poor Soul, Reggie Van Gleason, Charlie Bratton, et cetera, in all of which Art and I played non-"Honeymooners" characters—Jackie was the heart and soul of the whole one-hour variety show.

He approved and sometimes even suggested the June Taylor Dancers' costumes and routines. He worked with our orchestra leader, Ray Bloch, on all the musical numbers, supervised the supervisors in lighting, sound, and direction, and was the final word on all phases of production. The producers, in the end result, produced what Jackie's theatrical intuition told him was right for the show.

Now this was unheard of on network television. Bob Hope and Red Skelton had years more mass entertainment experience. Let's face it, they were also better stand-up comics than Jackie, whose pre-TV Show Biz career had ranged from raunchy saloons to top nightclubs, plus forgettable hero's-friend's-friend roles in a few movies. But Columbia Broadcasting System had given him carte blanche to do a prime-time network hour almost completely on the strength of his year fronting a similar show to a much smaller audience at DuMont. Their trust in this breezy, brazen Broadway showboat to capture the nation's consciousness based on his invincible confidence and dominance of every area of the show's operation was as startling as it was complete.

Bob Hope had a brilliant comedic mind and a flippant delivery, which built a throwaway gag into a roar, but he never claimed to be a lighting expert. Red Skelton was a flawless Clem Kadiddlehopper and Mean Widdle Kid, but he didn't compose musical bridges, or supervise audio feedlines or edit his shows.

Only Milton Berle had had such vast authority over his production. But Milton, for all his talent, didn't go on to compose, arrange, and direct inspiring music which sold millions and millions of albums. And Jackie did that when he couldn't read a note of music. He laid out the melody on the trumpet and had an arranger score it. You could say he had a shade of difference going for him.

He never discussed with me how he landed the CBS job which made his career and the extraordinary freedom to do whatever he wanted to make it the number-one show in the country. Naturally, I've heard a lot of unfounded stories of how he leaped over the moon from DuMont to CBS and stardom and riches (with all the stage privileges of the King Emperor), but I think the one told me by Phil Cuoco, our peerless scenic designer, who was with Jackie from Du-Mont to CBS to CBS Florida to forever, was most likely.

It seemed that CBS President William Paley and his wife, Babe, had dropped into Toots Shor's restaurant, a popular watering hole, for dinner. A well-oiled Toots invited himself to their table and began extolling the greatness of his pal Jackie Gleason, who was killing the people at DuMont, and if Bill Paley was smart and swift, he might just lure him over to CBS. Toots, with the drop taken, could be most convincing and, since he also was a giant, more than somewhat overwhelming. Supposedly, Mr. Paley became very smart and very swift between the soup and entrée and decided he would accept such sage advice with many thanks. He bought Jackie's contract the next day, and *The Jackie Gleason Show* featuring "The Honeymooners" became national television's number-one show for three straight years.

Close-up and slow dissolve to muted trumpet mellow in the middle distance torching "Our Love Is Here to Stay," the theme of "The Honeymooners."

Had to be that way.

★ SNAPSHOT ★

oots Shor's restaurant on West Fifty-second Street was both convenient and convivial to Mr. Gleason. He liked the host, the patrons, the atmosphere, and the liquid refreshments. Toots's famous line was "A bum who ain't drunk by midnight ain't trying," and some of the great names in sports, entertainment, business, and politics used to spend hard hours in the trying.

Jackie's friendship with Toots must have begun at the old Club 18. Toots had started as a bouncer, done well, and opened one of the most popular restaurants in New York, known for hearty food—steaks, chops, huge slabs of roast beef, and so on. Before Jackie struck it rich, he used to patronize Toots's because Toots would carry him on the cuff.

Toots said to me, "How do you like that bum?" (Toots's favorite term of endearment used only for those he loved). "He'd come in here with his friends, dead broke, order everything in the house, and when the check came, he'd sign with a big flourish, leaving a large tip for the waiter and captain, and I'd have to give them the tip! At one time, he was into me for over $10,000. I gotta hand it to him, though, when he got into the big money, he came by and handed me the cash, saying, 'Here's what I'm sure I owe you.' "

I used to go to Toots's a lot. One night he told me a

★ 51 ★

couple had come in from Omaha and complained to him bitterly about their steaks. They said, "We have much better steaks than this in Omaha." Toots, ever the genial host, said, "So what? When you're through eating, you're still in Omaha!"

Possibly inspired by the ranks of New York professional athletes sharing the festive board one night, Jackie suggested that Toots and he have a race around the block for double or nothing on the bill. A race between two men of such girth that the tying of their shoes required planning and stamina had the patrons loud in their comments, none of which will be repeated here. Jackie had only one stipulation. If they both ran in the same direction, a cop might take out the two of them, thinking he had felons fleeing the scene.

Jackie would run west on Fifty-second, north on Sixth Avenue, east on Fifty-third, south on Fifth, and west on Fifty-second to the restaurant. Toots would do the same course in reverse. There is no record of any bets being laid by the gambling crowd at the bar as the sprinters took their marks and then hurled themselves down the sidewalks. Pedestrians leaped for cover, rarely having seen fat, middle-aged men charging down the street, running either from or to cardiac arrest.

Glider Gleason flagged a taxi on Sixth and sank into the backseat as they covered Fifty-third and pulled up halfway down the block at Fifth. Five bucks for a one-block ride was aces with the hackie. Swifty Shor panted to his door, only to find Jackie toasting him with his own Scotch.

When Toots finally could breathe again and the blood returned to his brain, he recalled that he had not passed or been passed by Jackie at any time in the race. Toots never used foul language, but he came close that night. Jackie paid. He never said whether it was doubled or not.

★ SNAPSHOT ★

Comedy writer Leonard Stern had met Jackie when Gleason was second man in a just starting Las Vegas. Jackie wanted to lure the very best writers he could to do his network spot and began to weave all the ties of a very loose friendship to woo Stern from his Hollywood base to New York as a writer for *The Jackie Gleason Show,* with special responsibility for "The Honeymooners" skit.

Leonard was his "dear pal, his old buddy. Friendship really means everything in this business," et cetera and et cetera.

Following arduous long-distance courting, Stern agreed. "But, Jackie, I'll have to support two households if I take the job, one in California, one in New York," he pointed out. "I've got to get paid a thousand dollars a week to do that."

Jackie's awesome wrench of pain at such a monumental writer's salary (for 1952) echoed through the phone system, but Leonard was firm, and Jackie insisted on having the best.

"Okay, Leonard, you got it," Jackie agreed. "But we're not friends anymore."

Alice,
You're the Greatest

If anyone in the fifties had suggested to us that *The Honeymooners* would still be being telecast to generations yet unborn when we finished shooting it, he or she would have been told to stay comfortable until the people from Bellevue arrived to start their vacation. We were not creating drama for the ages but turning out fast-paced action, tightly plotted scripts, and broadly drawn characters, which the audience found endearing as well as comical. All this was possible because of our great writers.

Comedians and actors, when they're feeling beneficent, are wont to publicly thank everyone from the boom operator to the wardrobe mistress for making the show possible, usually neglecting to mention that if the writers hadn't provided inspired imagination, with sure stagecraft and a credible plot, the audience would have been treated to an evening of organ music

We had six top writers who wrote "The Honeymooners" and most everything else too. Their memory lingers on, along with their style and wit. Say hello to Walter Stone, Syd Zelinka, Marvin Marx, Leonard Stern, A. J. Russell, and Herb Finn. Plus Harry Crane, who wrote for *Cavalcade of Stars* and the first year of *The Jackie Gleason Show* before going on to a very successful Hollywood career. Al Schwartz joined us later. You guys can put words in my mouth forever.

It was Harry Crane, a fellow Brooklynite, who told me he had spotted Jackie in a local amateur show many years before and liked him and his antic humor. Harry recommended him to agent Willie Webber, who represented the young comic for years. He used to tell us how Jackie scored big at Jack White's Club 18 as one of four comics whose act was to sit on a bare stage and insult the audience. A dear man and a good friend, Harry Crane.

Like cloistered monks, the writers were kept in strict seclusion, and I well recall my early learning days, wandering about the Park Sheraton office complex and discovering a small staircase leading to the second floor. I could hear voices and typewriters going, so I walked up the stairs to find a dead-bolt lock on my side. I unlocked it and found it was the writers' office. One of them came down and sat with me in the living room to visit when suddenly Lee Reynolds, Jackie's svelte and imperious secretary, appeared, looked at the writer, and said, "How did you get in here?" Without a word, he scurried back up the stairs, and she turned on me. "Did you open that door?"

Sheepishly, I said, "Yes," not thinking I had done anything wrong.

In case I was imbecilic, she stated firmly, "Never touch that door again!" Needless to say, I made my exit with quite extraordinary ideas about what Miss Reynolds might do with that door and much of the Park Sheraton Hotel.

Love, Alice

Jackie being Jackie, ordinary rules of artist-writer co-operation did not prevail. The writers were locked away in their own particular area to conjure up misadventures in Bensonhurst for the Kramdens and the Nortons, and Jackie wouldn't even look at the completed script until Friday, the day before the show. I would hang around their door about 10:00 A.M. each Tuesday through Thursday like an orphan outside a bakery window. Abruptly, the door would open, and a hand would extend a single sheet of script, two if they were running hot. Delighted, I would pore over this gift, having no idea how the bit would develop in later install-ments but pleased that I had an inkling of what we were to do before millions of people in just a couple of days. In all honesty, this only went on for the opening weeks before I prevailed on Jack Hurdle, the producer, or Jackie himself (I forget which one) that this was one helluva way to run a railroad, much less a network television show.

Strangely, a gregarious Jackie kept his own relationship with the writers to far less than the bare minimum. If he had a suggestion or story idea, he would transmit it through the executive producer, Jack Philbin, rather than drop in and chat about it himself.

Writer Leonard Stern (now a successsful producer), a tall, handsome man and a valued friend, always considered Jackie's absence from the writers as positive—showing Gleason had total trust in his writers.

Somewhere along the line Jackie had acquired the rep-utation of not getting along with writers. Leonard feels almost the contrary is true. Jackie removed himself from the writers but this did not preclude his being a good editor.

Jackie was really ambivalent toward the writers. He hated being dependent on them, but he admired them. His trust was so great he did exactly what was written every

Saturday. He never violated the script. The only time any-one ad-libbed was if a prop broke or someone forgot a line—but the ad-lib was always in character. The cast never let the audience in on a mistake.

Jackie's relationship with the writers could not have been too bad because "The Honeymooners" had the least turnover of writers of any show. Most were with it for five to seven years. Leonard viewed Jackie as that rare come-dian—a noninterfering one—and really only saw him on Saturday, show day.

Stern and his writing partner, Syd Zelinka, found the confines of the hotel too restrictive and finally got Jack-ie's permission to work in a little apartment only five min-utes away. The employer-employee relationship became strained, however, because, for some reason, Jackie thought that Leonard and Syd were taking strolls in nearby Central Park when they should have been working. Words were ex-changed, temperatures rose between parties of the first part and those of the second part. The employer had neither wit-ness nor probable cause to buttress his opinion, but he was also the judge and jury.

One day Jackie called them and said, "Come over right away." They rushed to the Park Sheraton, since they had said they were only five minutes away.

He said, "What's the matter with you guys? Here I have a nice office for you and you won't use it. I think you're going for walks in the park instead of writing."

Both men said, "Jackie, we're not walking in the park."

Jackie continued with "I think the view from that apart-ment is conducive to walks in the park."

Leonard and Syd: "We are not walking in the park."

Jackie: "I want you to come in the office. You don't get story lines walking in the park."

Leonard and Syd: "Honestly, we don't take walks in the park."

Jackie: "Okay, you don't take walks, but I think you do."

Back to the Park Sheraton went happy and unmollified Leonard and Syd.

Not long afterward, with a nice fire going in the fireplace, they were working hard on a difficult script, with Syd puffing manfully on his omnipresent pipe. Leonard didn't notice the fog of fumes—he was so used to his partner's smoking—but the New York City Fire Department did. They appeared in slickers complete with gas masks and axes, pumpers and hook and ladders at curbside. The firemen eventually and grudgingly accepted the theory that one man could blow so much smoke that it looked like the building was on fire, but it is unknown whether Leonard and Syd's employer was persuaded. To be fair, Jackie never mentioned the word *arson*. Out loud.

At the start of each show, Jackie would stride down center stage all the way to the apron as the June Taylor Dancers unfolded about him in a mini-Ziegfeld opening. He would then lead off the frolics, with some of the most uneven comedy monologues performed since two-a-day Keith Orpheum circuit vaudeville. The writers had labored long to create fresh and clever gags to fit his delivery and style, yet, invariably, with five or six minutes to go, Jackie would find their words unacceptable and demand new stuff as the assistant director was ready to start his countdown and the Taylor girls were taking their places. (The writers referred to these mad-mumbles remade minutes as their Humiliation Festival.) All their honed, self-contained jokes were condemned, and they were required to come up with five or six thigh slappers during the overture.

George Jessel, a raconteur of humor for most of everybody's lives, was on one night and shared two stories with Jackie to help him out with his monologue. Jackie didn't think they were funny either. Who informed Jessel he could tell a joke?

Jackie had such confidence in his audience, he once pulled the office receptionist, Patty Raymond, a cute, petite girl, out onstage to tell this joke. "Man goes into a hat store, says, 'I want a hat.' Salesman says, 'Fedora?' The man says, 'No, for me.' " Gleason turned to the audience and said, "Look what I have to put up with."

Yet somehow, some way, he romped his way through the monologue, building a weak story, with antic facial tics and a voice which alternatively whispered and growled, and the audience ate it up.

I don't think any of us truly realized what an exceptional actor Jackie was in the early days of "The Honeymooners." Of course, he was a facile comic actor; that's all we saw at that time. He made himself into the role somehow, whether the role was what the audience thought a big-city hotshot like Jackie Gleason would say or do or even how he'd walk or gesture. Or a Brooklyn bus driver desperate for a better life for him and his Alice.

His two men about town—the pair of Jacks, Philbin and Hurdle—couldn't keep up with the bachelor pace Jackie set. Besides, they had wives who told them that they couldn't and shouldn't and wouldn't play perpetual boys' night out, so each took a night in turn so they could kiss their wives and remember how their homes looked.

But all three participated in one last bit of tomfoolery with Our Audrey cast as the fool. This was early in the first year I was on "The Honeymooners" and, at the time, unnerving, since I didn't know any of them very well.

One Friday night, I'd just finished washing my hair and

As a little girl in China.
Check the hat—it was
fashionable then.

All grown up in New York.

From the Bob and Ray show:
me as Whistler's Mother,
patiently waiting for
Whistler's Father to come
home from the saloon.

With Bob and Ray,
playing their version
of Duplication.

DUPLICATION

How to win a beauty contest Bob and Ray style: enter from every city.

★ ★ ★ ★ ★

How Audrey became Alice: I had these photos taken to convince Jackie
I wasn't "too pretty" to play a Bensonhurst housewife.

BILL MARK

BILL MARK

BILL MARK

BILL MARK

Alice: "Can I play through?"

Nothing scared Alice, not even
Ralph's flying finger of fate.

★ ★ ★ ★ ★

CBS

Breaking up at rehearsal, which was as much fun for us as the show.

Typical Jackie—he'd pose with the script, but not rehearse with it.

Playing Reggie Van Gleason's girlfriend in satin and ermine was a far cry from Alice in her housedress and apron.

Photo session: Jackie, Art, and Aud.

The great minds of comedy gather for the weekly production meeting. Left to right: Walter Stone, Marvin Marx, choreographer June Taylor, Jackie (with crutches, having broken his leg on the air), producer Jack Hurdle, writers Syd Zelinka and Leonard Stern.

★ ★ ★ ★ ★

Jackie watches a rehearsal on the monitor. Stanley Poss is to his left, Jack Hurdle to his right.

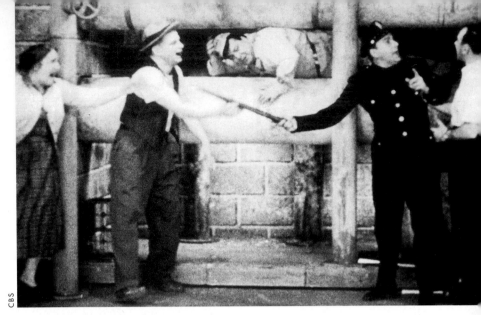

In this scene Jackie played Ralph in a tight squeeze. The only problem was, he really got stuck! Zamah Cunningham is on the left.

At rehearsal with our crew, who were our best fans and kindest critics.

was studying my script, which, thank God, had been delivered early, when Jackie called me in a panic. "Audrey, you've got to come over to my place right away. We have big script problems for the show tomorrow, and I need you to work them out. It's very important!" And more of the same.

I said, "Jackie, it's late. Can't we handle any changes tomorrow morning? I'm washing my hair, I'm a mess, my hair is soaking wet. . . ." But he was insistent, and strident. He'd never called me before like this, so I had to figure he was really worried. I said, "Okay, I'll be right over." Levi's, fur coat, tennies, and a towel for a turban, I responded to the call, and my knock on the penthouse door was answered by a straight-faced Jack Hurdle, who scurried off toward the kitchen, where Jack Philbin was glimpsed smuggling smiles with both hands. There was Jackie sitting on a couch at the far end of the room, facing the entrance. He gave a bashful grin as I approached the couch across from him. As I rounded the furniture to sit down, I saw skimpy bras, silk stockings, panties, and so on, scattered on the couch. I absorbed this shock with no change of expression. "What's the problem?" I stammered.

"Well, Audrey," he said, "it really wasn't the script. It's just that I've redone the living room, and I wanted to get your impression of how the decorator's ideas worked out."

It was only then that, looking at Jackie, I noticed that the floor lamp beside his couch had a quite extraordinary resemblance to a naked woman whose head was covered by a lampshade. Canting my head slightly, I saw that her twin was on the other side, both in place of the normal floor lamps. The fact that there were three men in the apartment and three women (only one clad) caused me a massive surge of apprehension. What is he trying to pull? went through my head. Am I being auditioned for an orgy?

Upset and confused, I tried flippancy before flight. I said, "Well, Jackie, I really can't see that you've done anything different with the place at all. Looks pretty much the way it always does."

"Oh, Aud," groaned Jackie, "you just don't get the joke. Come on, girls, she's a clam, no sense of humor." In Jackie idiom, being a "clam" meant you were a stiff, nonreactive, not with it, as close to unconscious as you could be while remaining vertical.

The human lamps doffed their shades and plunked down beside Jackie, regarding the only woman in the room with her clothes on somewhat quizzically. I departed with a cool "Good night," and an embarrassed Philbin left the kitchen to open the door for me. "I'll see you to the elevator," he said.

I said, "You'll do more than that. You'll figure out what bar we can go to where a woman in tennis shoes, a fur coat, and a towel around her head would be served, so we can have a little discussion about this performance."

I was really boiling. This was the kind of prank you'd expect from a bunch of drunken college kids, not three sober, grown men. We found a little, dark bar on Lexington Avenue. "Whatever made you think I would be amused? It's insulting, disrespectful, embarrassing, and about as funny as a crutch. If I'm going to work on this show, we have to get some things straight right now," and on and on. Philbin agreed with everything I said, which was most annoying. He said, "I assure you, Jackie will never mention this again! He will be more embarrassed than you!" I left soon after, telling him not to forget to put out the lights. Or did I say lamps?

A few weeks later, at rehearsal, I was sitting in the audience with Jack Philbin, when a tall, statuesque girl came down the steps from the stage. She was wearing a huge black hat and looked very glamorous. She said hello to me as she passed, so I said hello. Philbin said, "Who's that?"

"I've no idea. I've never seen her before in my life."

"But you said hello," he insisted. "Are you sure you haven't seen her before?"

"I'm positive!" But smelling a rat, I took another look. "Oh, my God, she's one of the lampshades, isn't she? You rat!" So they'd put me on again.

The nutty presequel (if there is such a word) to all this was, when I asked dear Phil Cuoco to remind me of any stories about Jackie I might have forgotten, he recounted how Jackie loaded Phil Napoleon's jazz group on the crack Detroiter train from Grand Central when he went out to open the Henry Ford Auditorium. Phil was dismayed he wasn't included in the group, but two days later came a wire for him to fly to meet the gang at the old Book-Cadillac Hotel. Phil followed the bellboy to the room, where he flicked the light switch to find two nudes in each corner of the room with the obligatory lampshades on their heads. The rest of the gala party descended on the room at that moment, and Phil tactfully drew a veil of modesty. Now I know why I didn't laugh when Jackie pulled his tired gag on me. Eight naked anything might be funny, two are just vulgar.

As I have explained before, Jackie never said anything bawdy or racy to women cast members in all the years I worked for him, with two exceptions . . . and they were said to me.

At rehearsal one day, we were crossing the stage from opposite directions, and as Jackie approached he said, "I've been thinking, Aud. I know it'll never happen, but if we ever did do it, we'd have to do it in the kitchen." This remark was about as risqué as Jackie ever got with me, or any other woman on the show, as far as I know. (Jackie's other racy line? It's under *F*, for *Fatchamara Matzarone*, later.)

Good fortune certainly smiled on me to become a part of this show at this particular time. It was obvious to all that "The Honeymooners" sketch was the favorite of the audiences, and Jackie and CBS and whoever minded the room where they kept all the money decided to lengthen it from twelve or fourteen minutes to thirty; later it became a full-hour show.

In 1990, I was interviewed on NBC-TV by Bob Costas, who is not only one of the most perceptive interviewers I've ever met but also one of the most knowledgeable and dedicated fans of "The Honeymooners." He observed that Alice was much more acerbic in earlier (and shorter) episodes. Of course, he was right. The pace had to be almost feverish to introduce the plot elements, establish the conflict while entering and exiting supporting players, resolve the conflict, and close.

Originally, "The Honeymooners" was played as sketch comedy, which I always think of as loud and fast, because it was only about nine or twelve minutes and we really didn't have time to establish depth or character. It wasn't until the writers got more time to develop the characters, as well as the action, that the Kramdens could show their love for each other and gain a kind of empathy from their national audience.

It was, of course, a comedy, but one with heart. Ralph was not an oaf, and Alice was not a shrew. Like everyone else, they were striving to make their lot a little better. My dear mother was so shocked at the Kramden shouts and insults of the early shows that she asked me to tell Mr. Gleason it wasn't nice to yell so at each other. In that first year, her response to friends who asked, "What is Audrey doing?" was a vague, "Oh, she's studying." But she grew to be a great fan. And years later she said, "You know, I think the reruns are even better." My mother was an adorable Billie Burke type. By this time she was reconciled to the fact that her daughter would not be twirling through a door à la Loretta Young.

The writers had two golden rules they never altered in writing the series:

1. The Alice character only responded when justified by Ralph's remarks. She never attacked.
2. The characters remained credible and plausible. There would not be purely exploitive episodes, i.e., running for Congress, joining the circus, swimming to Staten Island.

You get the idea.

Incidentally, when Jackie was asked by journalists what he thought was the secret of the show's success, his candor was deliberately unprofound. "Because it's funny," said the man who made it so.

"What is comedy?" he was asked.

"I don't know," Jackie replied.

No one, including Freud, who spent about 300 boring pages trying, has ever explained, to my satisfaction, what comedy is. If you're lucky enough to be gifted, and I don't mean that to sound immodest, it's a gift that's given to you. You just use it and don't try to do too much self-examination. To me, comedy timing is like music. There's a rhythm to it that is sort of in your bones. I don't know how you could teach it.

"The Honeymooners" standing set of the Kramden apartment would make a dungeon look like a *House Beautiful* profile, but there were reasons for its simplicity. Jackie's father had (in New Yorkese) "copped a walk" when he was nine years old, leaving his mother and himself destitute. His mother, Mae, lived a tough life as a change maker in the BMT subways, and the Gleasons moved often, and not upward, through the cheapest apartments in Brooklyn's Bushwick section. The Kramdens lived at 328 Chauncey Street, supposedly in Bensonhurst, but Jackie had lived on the real Chauncey Street in Bushwick, with no wage earner dad, in the rocks of the Depression, and he needed no set designer to tell him how the place looked.

Remember, there wasn't any telephone on the set. Nor, of course, in Jackie's Bushwick rooms. There was little furniture, a weary icebox (no refrigerator), a tiny sink, and that dominant table, stage center. If such surroundings didn't offer the strongest impetus in the world for Ralph Kramden to get lucky, to grab for a star, an idea, a gimmick, to lift Alice and himself to a better life, he was a zombie. And Ralph Kramden was no stiff. He was out there every Saturday with an angle, a scheme, an effort. You could laugh at him, but you had to cheer for him too. I'm sure I didn't know then, but I have since read psychiatrist Karl Menninger's dictum "Anything which can be made funny must have at its heart some tragic implications."

In all my years with Jackie, I only recall him giving me one bit of direction. A telegram was to be delivered to our door. "Aud," he said, "when you get it, look very worried." Discussing this years later with a good friend as Bronx Irish as Jackie was Brooklyn, I learned the reason for Jackie's advice. Very few even middle-class people had home telephones in New York in the thirties. A telegram was a notice of disaster. Surely a relative was dead or dying. My friend recalled his family receiving a telegram and his mother and father apprehensively passing it back and forth. Finally, it disclosed that his mother's brother's wife had just had a baby. His parents were more angry at being scared half to death by the menace of the telegram than joyful about the newborn. Jackie knew that such vulnerability had to be expressively played. A telegram, to the Kramdens, was an ominous event rather than an exciting occasion.

I can't recall Jackie ever giving Art Carney any directorial pointers, except once. An established move for Norton was to explore the Kramden icebox for food. Jackie added a great bit for him—since Art was alone onstage, Jackie said, "Art, when you close the icebox door, take your handkerchief and make a big move to wipe off the fingerprints." It got a huge laugh. He also gave one of his jokes to Art, saying it would be funnier coming from him. That's the mark of a true professional and a big star. Onstage, Jackie and Art seemed to think as one person, with timing, moves, stage businesses, even postures blending. They stimulated each other. Art was from a Yonkers Irish family of many sons. That misshapen fedora sported by Ed Norton actually was an Art Carney high school hat. Art noted that at his family's house, "there was always food on the table," indicating that luxuries were in short supply. Jackie treasured him both as a pal and as a talent, but they really didn't see much of each other outside work. Jackie loved to party, and Art didn't drink. Jackie lived the bachelor life in Manhattan, and Art had a wife and family in the suburbs.

Joyce Randolph and I liked each other, worked well

together, and still meet today, but I doubt if either of us knew the address of the other during the show. This was not at all unusual. For instance, one June Taylor dancer might have been single and lived in Greenwich Village and her best buddy married and commuted from Massapequa, Long Island. Cast and crew worked as close as family but rarely shared a social life off the set. In my experience, a cast hangs around together mostly when you're on the road. You don't know anybody in town. You want to grab supper with some company so the local hotshots will let you eat your chopped steak à la maison without having to block passes from guys who want to show you the town. Starting with their room.

Jackie, in practice to be the perpetual motion machine, shifted into high when the sun went down and he put the carnation in his buttonhole. It was off to bright lights, brassy music, and gifts which Fortune may hold hidden for adventurers such as himself. Jackie drank. Jackie drank lots. Lots and lots. I don't know whether he liked to drink or he just liked to be with people and at places where drinking was a reason for being there. He certainly didn't drink on the job in the fifties. I was closer to him than anyone else for years onstage, and I never smelled alcohol on him. He didn't have time the rest of the day, checking everything from light cues to dance steps.

I have also heard some awesome stories of alcohol consumption by him which would have rivaled the capacity of most TVA dams. But he was always there show day, bouncy, cheery, involved. If he had a hangover commensurate with the Scotch he was supposed to have downed, his next morning's buck-and-wing was the greatest acting since Junius Brutus Booth.

So, everyone was off for Levittown or Teaneck or Jackson Heights or to pick up the kids from the sitter or get a rinse and set. Except Jackie. Inside his head was a neon sign flashing **PLAY TIME.** And it's no fun to play alone. Producers Jack Philbin and Jack Hurdle plus Bullets Durgom were enlisted as fellow men about town.

In the early days of the first year when the script was late arriving on Friday, I would be recruited with a call from Jack Hurdle or Jackie. It was a very pleasant evening but became a very late evening. Dinner was delicious. Jackie cracked us all up with a running commentary of preposterous suppositions about the other guests. Following a couple of after-dinner stops at piano bars, where Jackie brought prosperity to the pianists, we arrived at a Dixieland place in the Village. Trumpets wailed and trombones moaned as waiters rushed to keep up with the bar orders for Mr. Gleason's table.

One particular Friday, glancing at my watch, I was shocked to learn we had left the evening a long time ago and were fast nudging the early morning away. Since Jackie never wanted anyone to leave when hearts were high and glasses raised, I said I was going to the ladies' room. I grabbed a cab and went home to study my script, which was waiting under my door. Not easy at 3:00 A.M. Fortunately, our rehearsal calls on Saturday were always 1:00 or 2:00 P.M. in the theatre, so I got some sleep. Jackie and pals were perfect gentlemen and witty and wonderful fellows, but if I'd made a habit of staying up late and drinking with them, I would have looked like Ma Kettle in six months.

So, when Jackie invited me on another night out, I quickly invented a special date.

Jackie said, "Great, Aud, bring him along."

I said, "I don't want to confuse him by going out with you guys, and this might turn out to be something pretty special. We'd rather be alone."

Jackie was a sucker for romance and assured me he

understood and wished me all good things. Yes, I did feel like some kind of a heel and was not pleased with myself. However, it was better than saying "Jackie, you're great, but six months of perpetual happy hours with you and The Boys and I won't be fit to play in a Punch and Judy." So I got undressed. I made a big bowl of popcorn and a pan of fudge, and got into bed to watch TV until the doorbell would announce that the script had arrived. That became my M.O. for succeeding Friday nights.

"The Honeymooners" had grown so popular with the public in *The Jackie Gleason Show* that CBS wanted more of it. My old pal Bullets Durgom realized he had boxed me into an every-other-week contract. The MCA agency suddenly discovered they had no hold on me. I could leave any time I got a better offer. So Bullets directed Val to have me sign a weekly contract. I said, "No, thank you, I'm happy the way I am." Bullets enlisted the thunder and lightning of MCA, mover and shaker of entertainment planets. I said, "No, thanks. You didn't trust my work enough to sign me for the whole season, so you could dump me without paying off if it didn't work out. So I'll just keep things the way they are."

Since I was single, and MCA being MCA, they sent around an agent who looked as if he were from central casting himself—if not the most handsome man in the world, he was in the semifinals—to take me out. He expounded the company line, which was how I had to sign for my own security. I said, "You mean your security," and let him walk my poodle when he visited while I, presumably, considered "my security." Pierrot, my poodle, liked him. So did I. But I didn't sign. Yet. Jackie didn't know then that they didn't have me locked in, and he didn't know until the last show of that first season.

★ SNAPSHOT ★

A feature of *The Jackie Gleason Show* was tight close-ups of the marvelous faces of a corps of Manhattan's most beautiful models called—so help me—the Glea Girls. Each lady had a face you could put on a stamp. High cheekbones, perfect nose, alluring full lips, skin which had never seen a single zit, eyes that glowed in the dark. Naturally, their hair and eyebrows and lashes and makeup were applied by artists. If you can have knockout earlobes, the Glea Girls had earlobes to die for. But Jackie, a man who admired women and also liked them, which often are two different things, had a serious problem with the goddess group.

They couldn't smile.

For some unknown reason, fashion photographers in those days seemed to require magazine models and fashion show mannequins to adopt a contemptuous look somewhere between a pout and a sneer as they posed their size-six bods. If you could show disdain without wrinkling your nose as if you smelled a garbage scow, you were *Vogue* cover girl material.

Well, *The Jackie Gleason Show* was a variety show, and it included pretty girls. Mr. Gleason considered that an unsmiling girl was as pretty as a passport picture. He would teach each of these beauties to grin like a Cheshire cat if it killed him, or them.

They would peep an incisor, give you a quick look at uppers hugging lowers in a halfhearted try, but then clamp down obedient to the fashion gurus, who had told them scorn conquers all. Jackie, though, could get most of them giggling. If he could make America laugh, he certainly could get a Glea Girl to open her mouth and chortle. Once he got them to laugh, he could tutor them in smiling. Some, not all.

"Aud," he said to me, "you know why models are so thin? I just found out. A lot of them don't have any teeth!"

★ SNAPSHOT ★

Our writers were inventive enough to work any un-planned happening into a "Honeymooners"' script. Jackie himself came to the rescue with a great line for me when I discovered I was allergic to shrimp, which I had eaten before the show. One of my eyes blew up like a bal-loon. It swelled so badly, my eyebrow was pushing up to my hairline. I ran to Jackie, who had had a similar experience with shellfish. They got a doctor to give me a shot of adren-aline, and he ordered a black eye patch for me to wear.

Here's what Jackie created for my black eye patch per-formance:

> **TRIXIE:** What happened to your eye?
> **ALICE:** I forgot to do the laundry.
> **TRIXIE:** So?
> **ALICE:** Ralph threw his socks at me.

★ SNAPSHOT ★

Joyce Randolph (Our Trixie) had met her husband-to-be, Dick Charles, when we were working out of the Adelphi Theatre later. Their romance rose in tempo and temperature apparently unknown to Jackie.

One day we were grabbing lunch at Al & Dick's, a great steak and chop place across from the Adelphi. There were Joyce and Dick lost in each other's arms so completely that their steaks were becoming overcooked on the plates from their combined heat.

A startled Jackie was embarrassed by this public midday demonstration of purple passion. When we assured him that marriage was just around the corner for the lovebirds, he decided to play genial boss instead of unlikely prude.

Recalling, I believe, the problem they'd had replacing Pert Kelton with me in the role of Alice, he dropped a note on the table as we left the swooning Joyce and Dick. It read: "Okay, but no babies."

Mmmm, You're a Good Group

Why, you may wonder, was Audrey rocking the boat about contracts and such when "The Honeymooners" was going so well? Since you were rash enough to ask, I want you to know that I was thrilled with the success of the show. However, the history of theatre life had engraved on my spirit the fact that an actress may well receive fond pats and airy compliments and still be paid off in subway tokens on the fire stairs unless she represents clearly that she has made a contribution to the successful work and needs to be rewarded for her zeal and energy.

Actresses have traditionally been paid less than actors ever since Elizabethan producers switched from using boys to play Lady Macbeth and Juliet and let those of us who could pass the physical for the role play it. Yet the recompense for such demanding work has been more curtain curtsies than a living wage.

I am no hot-eyed feminist, in great part because I consider men altogether wonderful and appropriate companions for most public and all private occasions. I don't know what they would do without us, or what we would do without them, and, thank God, neither of us seems to have attempted to go it alone with any fervor. But the goals of any professional actress have a tendency to shift from misty dreams of ethereal stardom to concerns with food, clothing, and shelter. You must ask or you shall never receive.

Many of today's working women, whether in high tech or retail or assembly line, seem to think they will be recognized and promoted and rewarded by a form of divine osmosis. It will not happen, ladies. Wishing won't make it so. Men learned this a long time ago, and big executives are not shy about bare-knuckles bargaining. What do you think they invented lawyers for?

So I purposely bring up the harsh facts of television life while commenting on even such a wonderful group as "The Honeymooners." Relationships in creating and playing the show were the best I've ever experienced in any form of theatre. But when it came down to contracts (read: money), you had to deal with nonshow people who valued your stage work in the same way they would a magician's long-legged feminine assistant—decorative, but essentially nonessential. (I swear, they did talk like that.) While you had managers and agents in your corner, you knew they weren't going to go over the falls for you and then have to come back and fight the good fight for all the rest of their clients.

Before we knew it, we had come to the last show of the season and were looking forward to thirteen weeks of summer vacation. Jackie came to me and said, "Aud, I understand you haven't signed for next year, is that right?"

I said, "Yes."

He said, "Can we talk about it?"

"Sure," I said.

"Well, meet me in the Cordial Bar" (it was right next to the theatre and was everyone's meeting place). When we sat down, Jackie said he'd heard I was being difficult, asking for a lot of things.

I said, "Not true. I am only asking for a raise."

Surprised, he said, "Is that all, you're sure?"

I said, "Of course. What have they been telling you?"

He was so relieved, he said, "Well, then we've got a deal," and we shook hands on it.

Considering the matter settled, I went ahead with my summer plans to go to Europe with my good friend Lila King and her parents. Starting with Paris, then the South of France, we finally reached Venice, where I was having a ball. Then disaster—a wire came from my manager saying all hell was breaking loose in New York with MCA and Bullets. I would have to come home immediately and sign my contract. Leave Venice early? Miss Rome and Geneva? Horrors! After a good deal of thought, I sent a wire to Jackie saying, I THOUGHT WE MADE A DEAL IN THE CORDIAL BAR. IT'S UNFAIR TO ASK ME TO CUT MY TRIP SHORT.—LOVE, AUD. The return wire was typical. ALL IS WELL—STAY AND HAVE FUN. SEE YOU IN THE FALL—J.G. Can you blame me for loving this man?

All of us started to get fan mail as the show became a Saturday-night standout in all markets—big cities, suburbia, small towns—and in all regions of the country. A lot of CBS biggies exhaled a little, never quite sure that a New York City–oriented show by locale, characters, and colloquialisms would be accepted in that mysterious land west of the Hudson River.

I started to receive literally hundreds of kitchen curtains

and thousands of aprons. America's women were so sorry for me in that drab Bensonhurst apartment that they wanted to cheer it and me up a little. I got everything from dotted swiss and regal semidrapes to merry chintz with tiebacks. One dear lady must have thought Ralph and Alice were really up against it. She enclosed ten cents to buy a curtain rod, since, while she could buy one locally, it would be too awkward to mail.

The aprons ranged from dainty to dramatic, from lacy French maid to enveloping butcher boy. Personally, I never thought wardrobe ever gave me a classy enough dress to require an apron's protection. But, evidently, Jackie did.

Naturally, we donated all the gifts to charitable sources, who saw to it that the curtains and aprons brought a brightening effect to many, many kitchens, and we thanked our concerned contributors. A bank sent me pot holders, saying if I banked with them, Ralph would never know where my money was.

As the years went on, the fan mail was fantastic in volume and dear in warmth and friendliness. I've heard it said, and am convinced it's true, that television actors who are naturally viewed in the environs of your own home become almost familiar, as opposed to motion picture or stage actors, who are always viewed in the formal surroundings of a theatre. A "moon pitcha" star is someone who lives in a world apart. Alice Kramden was part of your living room every Saturday night.

Among the thousands of sweet and gentle letters I received, there were always a few from some lost souls with whom you would not wish to share a Saturday living room or indeed a public street. One fellow wrote me several times seeking aid. It seems he thought the CIA had planted an invisible microphone in his teeth. He was receiving all kinds of instructions and music through his molars. It was driving him to distraction. Could I help? No, I could not, but I was sure he could look under "Dentist" in the Yellow Pages and have the offending mike removed.

One sport was convinced that Himself and Myself were married and had a thriving, red-haired family whose adventures he reported in pages and pages of rich detail. This one got a trifle spooky. The New York City detectives narrowed the sender to someone in the Manhattan YMCA and actually walked in on him when he was composing yet another report on our kiddies. The cops thought he was flaky but not dangerous, and told him to break his pen point or else they would have a room for him which was not up to YMCA standards. He promised the game was over but confessed he had mailed one to me the day before. The detectives thought that showed basic honesty and directed him to write only to Santa Claus and the Elves in the future. He said he would, and he did.

But every actress is bound to get two or three obscene letters out of thousands, and I got mine. The wording was obscene, but the stationery was first class. In fact, it even had a fancy, embossed woman's name and address for a letterhead. Turned out it was the lady's husband, who was talking through his shorts. He explained that he used his wife's writing paper because she had tagged him at this hobby before and carefully counted how many sheets of his own stationery he used.

I had received a series of obscene telephone calls at my apartment, a very heavy breather who managed to get in a last mixed bag of filth before I hung up. These calls seemed to happen in cycles to a lot of actresses. But at least I was spared from any personal contact with these sick individuals. One actress arrived home to find someone had slashed all the clothes in her closet and left. So, I was content to settle for the heavy breather.

Over the five very close years of "The Honeymooners," Jackie and I chatted about anything and everything off the set, from his life and loves to mine, politics and sports, show business, and people we liked and didn't. He probably learned a lot about my early life, but he was vague about his own.

Times had been very hard for Jackie and his mother, Mae. I know he had been devoted to her and always wanted to achieve some form of greatness so that she could be proud of him and he could shower her with the good things. But she died, painfully and at home, before he had a chance to be more than just a neighborhood teenager with a most uncertain future.

He somehow flummoxed the New York City Board of Education to elude high school after graduating from the eighth grade at P.S. 73. He steered an erratic course to the very top of Show Business via becoming the local pool shark, then emcee of amateur nights in neighborhood Brooklyn movie houses, and finally of comedy spots in taverns, bars, and roadhouses where the audiences were as rough as the whiskey. He paid his dues over and over without any promise that he would ever ascend to that plateau where you rated a star on your dressing room door. Or a dressing room. Or a door. But he kept learning and growing.

Jack Carter had been the lead comic on DuMont's *Show of Shows* when he abruptly left. The show's producer called Bullets Durgom to see if he could find a replacement, like yesterday. Bullets called Jackie, who was making $250 a week in a West Coast gig where he could talk louder than the drunks in the audience. Bullets said he could get him $2,500 a week on *Cavalcade of Stars* if he could make it. He could make it. Jackie told me he was ready to sprint to the airport; he obviously was feeling able to run faster than the cab could drive.

For a guy with the bare basics of education and much of a professional life shared with those on the far, far edge of the culture circuit, Jackie had an amazing body of knowledge on a wide variety of subjects. The fact that he possessed both a quick mind and a photographic memory didn't hurt at all.

One area we both were interested in was parapsychology—why do things happen without rational or at least explainable causes, and the always fascinating world of what was beyond the conscious. We're not talking about ghosties and goblins here or séance patter but tantalizing clues that say: "There are more things in heaven and earth, Horatio, than are dreamt of in your philosophy."

Jackie was particularly fascinated by the challenges to and the proofs of a hereafter. What did we know and what could we know? Every clime and culture has some form of religion which seems strange or ludicrous or even profane to religionists of other persuasions. Yet virtually all promise reward or punishment forever depending upon how a personal life on earth measures up to the particular code of the particular religion. There are so many cults, so many codes. Is there a correct one, and, indeed, is there reward or punishment or just ending? That was Jackie's constant study.

Hell, Purgatory, and Limbo are Christian concepts, yet Jackie treasured a remark from a famous rabbi who had declared, "I do not worship God as a divine arsonist." Jackie believed in a merciful Jesus, not a vengeful Jehovah.

He was especially interested in an experience I had as a young stock company player with an event which reached beyond the mundane, not exactly into a Twilight Zone but into areas ungoverned by normal rules.

Lila King, my old friend who had been in *High Button Shoes* with me, joined me at the Paper Mill Playhouse in New Jersey for a summer stock run. We roomed together at a boardinghouse in town. Both of us liked to sleep with the windows open, but each morning we'd find the windows closed. This became very aggravating. Suspecting our landlady of tiptoeing in at night to close the windows in case of rain, we edged a bookcase across the door one night, so we could catch her as all the books tumbled out and awakened us.

Didn't help. The windows were closed tight again. They were French windows which cranked open with a handle, not a sash that could come loose and slide down—you really had to wind the handle to crank them shut. Perplexed, I began to study the books in the bookcase. I saw they were all boys' adventure books, which seemed odd. The Tom Brown series, and so on. We studied the room, trying to figure out how she did it—knocked on the wall to see if there was a hidden door, but on the other side of the wall was the bathroom, and the wall was solid.

I didn't tell Lila what I thought was the solution, but I went down to breakfast early the next morning. Mrs. Buhrer was our landlady, and I approached her as she was bent over the stove cooking breakfast. "What did your son die of in our room?" She froze, asked me how I knew. I told her about the windows and how we thought she was doing it. She sat down and told me of her little boy's death there some years before. I said, "Well, his spirit seems to have remained, nonthreatening, warm, comfortable. By closing the windows it seems as though he's trying to get your attention to let you know that although he's gone, maybe he hasn't gone so very far away." Mrs. Buhrer was happy. Me too.

All of us have had occasions of clairvoyance. You recall the event with momentary wonder and forget it five minutes later. Children seem to experience this more than adults, but it is universal. How can we have perception before we can perceive?

Another wild one that happened to me that Jackie had me tell over and over was a letter I received from Bill, a young intern who had taken care of me when I was ill at Columbia-Presbyterian Hospital in Manhattan. I had a wild crush on him.

After I had moved to California, I awoke one morning with an image in my mind, as clear as a photograph, of an envelope with the return address of Bethesda Naval Hospital in Maryland. Even though I'd had no contact with him since that hospital stay, I somehow knew that this was a letter from Bill.

You can imagine my shock when I went through the mail and there was the letter with the return address exactly as I had visualized it.

The letter was witty and friendly, but it wasn't the start of the Love of My Life. It was just a letter from a nice guy I'd seen months ago who had never talked to me about the navy or leaving New York. All of a sudden, I'm seeing a precisely return-addressed envelope on the morning I envisioned it. Curious? Sure. Normal procedure? Not by a long shot. Explainable? Most everything is, isn't it?

I'm going to take five before I start sounding like Fatima in the Gypsy Tearoom. But if I'm going to tell you something about Ralph Kramden without his bus driver's suit,

I've got to mention the fact that he was a probing, questing, concerned human being. He was interested in verities and mysteries which have been debated for thousands of years. He was far more than Fatso the Clown. He was an actor who could play a broad character with subtlety beneath the bombast, a musician who could compose tone poems without knowing how to read a note of music. He also was a very sweet guy to have around.

★ SNAPSHOT ★

"Fatchamara Matzarone" (or a reasonable facsimile) was the awesome call of an aggrieved or furious Gleason character in anguish or vengeance, which meant whatever Jackie wanted it to mean when he was in the profound business of Italianate blood lust or had merely squashed his thumb with a hammer. It always brought down the house.

Every New York studio audience knew elements of Italian or Yiddish slang, or they must have been visiting from Montana. So the people were reasonably aware that this syllabic jumble was just babble. But they probably also were aware of coarse language which was reasonably similar and would have aptly fit the horrendous occasion, so they appreciated the bombast and the futility of Jackie's jabberwocky.

Remember, comedian Sid Caesar would do entire skits in effusive Italian (lotsa vowels and arm waving), ersatz German (gutturals and heel clicks), fraudulent French (loose-lipped proposals of intrigue or inanity with sloppy oohs and aahs), and Japanese (sibilant hissings and frequent bowing), which was great comic acting and appeared accurate enough to be followed as the real thing.

When I was new to the show and innocent to his pranks, I asked Jackie what, if anything, *Fatohamara Matzarone* meant. He gave me an answer which measured how much I could blush. It became his game for a few weeks to stop me and say, "And there is another translation . . ." and start on some complex fable which would have me running for cover.

The joke ended when I had an Italian pal teach me a tortuous sentence which meant something like "May your hair net fall into the overalls of your third cousin" and had awesomely vulgar-sounding diphthongs. I sprang it on Jackie on his next rude explanation. It stopped Mr. Fatchamara cold and gained me wary respect and freedom from fictitious translations.

I, too, could say a mouthful, even though I didn't know what it was full of.

You're Gonna Get Yours

"The Honeymooners" was not only accepted by New Yorkers but was considered their own special slice of network television. Jackie's key lines, such as "Oh, you're a good group!" or "A little travelin' music," were adopted first by New Yorkers as a kind of inside language of the city. The menacing "One of these days" or "Alice, you're gonna get yours," followed by "Bang! Zoom! A trip to the moon, that's what you're going to get!" (which never fazed Alice in the least) became kidding idioms from penthouses to walk-ups. No one is really sure who wrote these, since Jackie put variations on them through the years.

Naturally, bus drivers seemed to have a particular regard for us, since "The Honeymooners" was probably the first time their jobs had ever received dramatic attention. I can't count the number of times I was enjoying a walk on Fifth Avenue or sitting on a crosstown street when a huge city bus would pull up beside me, the driver honking happily, asking me to hop aboard. Then the passengers would yell and applaud and wave as I tried to explain that I was just going a block, thanks. By this time, cars were starting to build up behind the bus, and their horns were honking, but not happily. This prompted the passengers to lean out the windows and shout and/or scream rude remarks at the offending cars. If they spotted a New Jersey license plate on any, their rudeness would become both bitter and personal. (New Yorkers don't seem to dislike people who live in New Jersey, except if they drive cars from there into their city.) Usually, I'd throw everybody kisses and duck into a store before mob action commenced. The same reaction also greeted Art and Joyce, except Art—whenever a manhole cover was open—would be invited into the sewer.

Manhattan had always been known for the legendary characters who drove the city's cabs. Streetwise, funny, great gabbers, they had encyclopedic knowledge of all the byways of the city and were pleased to be able to get you to your destination in jig time, in traffic which would have stalled a presidential motorcade. Alas, they must be all gone now, since the new cabbies don't seem even to know the names of the hotels, much less how to get to them. But here are a few instances of adventures in cabology during the fifties that I recall:

> **DRIVER:** You're the third celebrity I had today.
> **ME:** Oh, who were the other two?
> **DRIVER:** Milton Berle and Steve Allen.
> **ME:** (perplexed) Really?
> **DRIVER:** Actually, come to think of it, they got into the hack ahead of me. But you're my third.
> **ME:** My pleasure.

Love, Alice

Another driver had two thermoses up front and offered a choice of iced tea or iced coffee during the ride on a hot summer day. Columnist Dorothy Kilgallen had had an item about him in her *Journal-American* column, which I'd read, but he had a photocopy for me to scan anyway as I sipped the drive away. He talked and talked about his in-trip services, hot coffee in the winter, and famous people who had been fortunate enough to have been his passengers.

Evidently, I had been sipping and nodding without displaying proper enthusiasm, because he glanced over his shoulder at me and said, "Well, come on—converse. I've got to tell people what you said in my cab just to me."

I don't know what I said, just to him, but I did what I was told. He might have taken my iced tea back.

I'd waved down a cab one night, late for a dinner date, and knew I'd made a grievous error when I got in the backseat. This clunker must have been number one off the assembly line. It was dingy and noisy, and the driver thought he was Mario Andretti. I was uncomfortable. I would become more so. The driver appeared to rely more on his horn than on his brakes to navigate traffic. It now appeared we were speeding in what some might call the parking lane. I saw a station wagon double-parked at the curb and yelled, "Watch out!" Too late! I felt my practically peerless pilot run this mobile junker into the rear of the station wagon.

I saw no more. I was catapulted across the passenger compartment and was flat on my back with my legs jammed underneath the front seat. Struggling to sit up, since I couldn't release my legs, I found I could barely peep over the door as the driver barreled out of the car to angrily dispute with the station wagon owner and a doorman. I made appropriate mewling noises interspersed with calls for aid, or friendship, or is there a bonesetter who makes cab calls? The doorman and the hitee didn't know there was a passenger in the taxi because they obviously couldn't see anyone or hear me over the volume of passing traffic. And my driver had, obviously, more vital things on his mind. Time passed.

I don't know whether the driver heard my waiflike call during a pause in hostilities or whether he suddenly re-called the fare hadn't paid for the trip yet. But the door finally opened, and the driver observed me, slumped with bloody legs firmly jammed under the front seat. "Lady," he intoned reproachfully, "you'll have to get another cab!"

Jackie was stuck in traffic in a cab one day. As he be-came more and more frustrated he bellowed to the driver, "Can't you go any faster than this?"

"Sure I can, Mr. Gleason," came the reply, "but I'm not allowed to leave my cab."

Jackie's weight ranged between 180 and close to 280, which, as the fella says, is a far piece. It involved important haberdashery bills. He built three complete wardrobes to accommodate the erratic rhythm of his appetite. When he was celebrating in the evening hours, he put away enor-mous amounts of meats and groceries, according to witnesses. In part, I presume this was because he was, ob-viously, hungry. He also was convinced that food absorbs much of the effect of alcohol. Maybe it does, but it also created a lot more of Jackie.

Periodically, when he'd feel swollen with idle calories, Jackie would check himself into a hospital and go on a rigid diet. He survived on the seeds and twigs his diet doctor thought appropriate, but if anything he increased his nor-mal smoking from five or six packs a day to whatever he could get between his lips. He appreciated company, but, as his confinement lengthened, his temper shortened.

One day a couple of the writers dropped in, only to find the nurse making an empty bed and the master gone.

"Where's Mr. Gleason?" the nurse was asked.

"Oh, he felt sick," she explained, "so he went home."

Who would want to be sick in a hospital, right?

I fail to identify the writers involved because at least three of them have confessed that they were the ones who had this conversation, but it became Jackie Gleason lore within hours.

This story has been repeated ad infinitum.

Finally, Jackie discovered a Swiss physician who was internationally famous on the subject of diet. This doctor told him that the worst thing he could do for his body was to undergo these periodic crash diets, constantly thrusting drastic changes on his system. Being overly stout is not recommended, but it's better than debilitating the physical structure with constant ups and downs. Jackie loved this man. He could now shift to his extra-large closet forever.

Although Doctors Hospital was dietary home for Jackie, it also became the site for a series of one-on-one nocturnal escapades for Phil Cuoco, our peripatetic scenic designer. Jackie had advised hospital security that Phil was to have carte blanche access to his room. Very often at 11:00 P.M., Phil's phone would ring, and there would be the familiar voice. "How're ya, pal? Get up to the White Castle on Eighty-sixth Street . . . get three dozen everything-on-it hamburgers, an apple pie, and a pint of strawberry ice cream . . . and, pal, right away. What? Nah, don't worry about the night nurse, she's on our side, a real clam."

Phil had a close friend of many years, Art Zerol. Art was the expert designer of Lionel Train layouts and dioramas (department store Christmas lures for goggle-eyed children, a Lionel specialty). Art lived and worked in his studio, a turn-of-the-century house in the Old Chelsea section of New York.

Phil had introduced Art to the Great One since they had two things in common:

1. They loved trains.
2. Their parents had been too poor to buy them wind-up sets (Ives, American Flyer), or much more expensive Lionels.

Each time Jackie was incarcerated in the hospital, Art would build and supply, on the cuff, a bedside Lionel operating layout. Jackie would play engineer. When Jackie was medically sprung, the layout would be moved to the Park Sheraton penthouse. Ultimately, it would wind up at the Monsignor's Boys Club in Red Bank, New Jersey.

In New York and Hollywood, there was a practice in TV shows whereby if a performer could work in the name of the product with his dialogue, the company would send cases of the product as a gift. No money changed hands, just a year's supply of toothpaste, canned food, whatever. We all knew an advertising executive, Nelson Shraeder, who was one of many participants in providing products. The more blatant (or more artful) publicists were better known as schlockmeisters, and their genius for placing their products was imaginative and legendary. Broadcast Standards fought the good fight, but as far as I could see, the schlockmeisters were winning the war hands down.

Jackie, in the character of Reggie Van Gleason, always

featured booze. He loved the sound of "Old Smuggler"—felt it was a great saloon phrase. Nelson was not about to overlook this chance. Whenever Reggie took a belt and said, "Um boy, that Old Smuggler is good booze," Nelson would deliver three cases of it.

Jackie went back to the hospital for another diet try and again went the phone call to Phil. Direct quote from Phil:

> **JACKIE:** How're ya, pal? Get in a cab, go down and pick up Art Zerol for a meeting—stop at Eighty-sixth Street, pick up the usual goodies, and, pal, hurry up!
>
> **PHIL:** Jackie, do you know what time it is?
>
> **JACKIE:** Stupid, do you think I'd be calling if I didn't know the time? It's 1:30 A.M. . . . hurry up."

At the Meeting

> **JACKIE:** Broadcast Standards is making loud noises about the Old Smuggler plug. We need an out.
>
> **PHIL:** Some time ago in a conversation, Nelson told me his people would deliver on the word *booze*.
>
> **JACKIE:** That's our out!

At 4:00 A.M., the three heads are still grinding.

> **PHIL:** Art, could you make a track control to stop-start and control a locomotive and a couple of cars for a short run?
>
> **ART:** No problem.
>
> **JACKIE:** How about a water tower that delivers one shot of booze?

ART: No problem.
ALL THREE: (in unison) We got it! We got it!

The Jackie Gleason railroad consisted of a Lionel Pacific locomotive, a tender, a gondola car with three shot glasses, and a caboose. It ran from stage left to stage right, waist high, and was backed by an electrified water tower.

Jackie had button panel controls for start (forward), stop (tank), lower, pour, raise (spigot), and reverse. On the air, when Jackie removed the filled shot glass and took a belt, unknown to Phil or Art, he bellowed, "Um, that Lionel delivers good booze." It did. Nelson sent three cases of Johnnie Walker Black, but all hell broke loose.

It was near Christmas. The Lionel and CBS switchboards lit up like a Christmas tree. The network didn't wait for Monday to fire Phil. A Sunday-morning call informed him he'd been terminated. But Mr. Lionel Cowan, CEO of Lionel, called Bill Paley, CEO of CBS, and exclaimed that the bit had produced hundreds of kids' telephone orders for the "Gleason Booze Tower." No more were ever made, but Lionel was happy, and, once again, Phil was off the hook.

When he told Jackie he'd been fired again, Jackie blithely looked at him and exclaimed, "Pal, why are you always getting into these scrapes with the CBS brass?"

Phil loved reminiscing about Jackie and one day told me how he happened to get his job. It seems Frank Sinatra had been completely taken by Phil Cuoco's set management talents and wanted him on Frank's show from Hollywood. But Manhattan Phil had no yen for eating oranges off the tree when he could get the same juice at Nedick's, Chock Full O'Nuts, and even Childs in New York. At Shor's they even put sparkle in the orange juice. A disappointed Frank vigorously recommended Phil to friend Jackie as the man for him and his new CBS show.

Love, Alice

Summoned to appear before what might be his employer to be, Phil approached the session with the indecorous air of seasoned production experts who view the majority of stars as people with holes in their heads or their pants.

He arrived more than a trifle tardy to an executive double phalanx of self-important suits sitting in judgment on his skills and talent with Jackie in the lead chair. The evaluation was as follows:

> **JACKIE:** Is this the bum we've been waiting for?
> **PHIL** (to no one in particular): Who's the fat guy?
> **JACKIE:** Hire him.

Phil lasted the whole nine yards with *The Jackie Gleason Show* in every shape and form. He even went to Florida when Jackie was there. I don't know whether he likes the oranges there.

"Honeymooners" writer A. J. "Andy" Russell might have had a more profound awareness of what made Jackie think and act the way he did than the rest of us, because he was a Brooklyn neighborhood boy who had lived near enough to Bushwick to be a fellow member of the ghetto, "only we didn't call it that." But the first time the two of them actually met was when Andy was writing a *Studio One* drama starring actor Gleason.

Amazed to find that Jackie knew his lines cold on the first reading (we could have told him that), Andy soon discovered that he and Jackie had grown up "within spitting distance" of each other, making them instantly kindred spirits.

"Why don't you come and work for me?" suggested

Jackie on the spot. But Andy protested he was not a joke writer; he worked with dramatic situations.

"But that's what I want to develop with the Ralph Kramden character. He's a person, he's Everyman, not a stick figure whose life is just a collision of belly laughs." Jackie crowned the analysis with "Ralph is a moax" (rhymes with smokes).

Presumably a fellow Brooklyn homeboy knew what a moax was or aspired to be. Jackie used the term a lot, and only by accent or gesture did we have hint of what a moax might be. It wasn't derogatory, but it didn't signify greatness either. I guess Everyman might fit, but one never knew!

Paired with Herb Finn, Andy was to find that a good writer is a good writer—including a writer of jokes. He and Herb were responsible for the classic "The Golfer" script, which took place in Everyman's single-set Everyroom as Ralph and Ed utilized a manual to master the art of golf minus the greens, fairways, roughs, or sand traps. Ralph's getup was wild plus fours, massive tam-o'-shanter, and animated application to a sport which required the participant to dress in garish fashion to assault an inoffensive ball.

Ed maintained his customary sewer togs, along with his whimsical manner of exploring the novel world of golfdom. Both Ralph and Ed were baffled by instructions on how to "address" the ball. Ed solved the problem by assuming a driving stance, bowing gracefully, doffing his fedora, and offering the greeting "Hello, ball."

I've saved the moment with pictures of this gem of foolishness, which knocked out the cast and crew as well as the audience. A memorable showstopper.

Andy and Herb also composed our "The Man from Space" script, which had Ralph going to a costume party at the Raccoon Lodge as an extraterrestrial type who looked as if the only way he could disrobe would be with a can opener. The prize was fifty dollars. Naturally, Jackie took personal control of his weird wardrobe. Making his entrance covered in kitchen equipment, the icebox door, knobs from the bureau, and a pot on his head, he struck a pose—at which a piece of his costume fell off. I said, "You're losing it already," as I reached to pick it up. He said, "Give me that. I need it. That's my denaturizer." Pretty quick ad-lib.

It was thirty years later when I learned that a denaturizer is a substance added to alcohol to change it. Only a man with a thirst like Jackie's would know a word like that.

Andy, in long discussions with Jackie, considered that he had an instinctive sense of what would be funny and what would grow into expanded laughter by shifting from buffoonery to blandness, which, of course, highlighted the nuttiness of the original premise. But he also insisted that a structured premise was the pivot which supported and enhanced everything else. Comic acting is not an excursion in either droll wittiness or maniacal zaniness. It is a logical embroidery from circumstance or situation which is restructured into humor. Departures from the norm lead to all comedy.

Andy and his family lived in Westchester County, not too far from Jackie's massive igloo, which was also perhaps too close. (This was Jackie's custom-built house, which you'll read about later on.) Jack Hurdle and Jack Philbin were usually weekend companions of Mr. Gleason, but, come Monday, he grew lonely and required companionship and action. While Jackie was an omnivorous and fast reader, he grew bored when he considered that being alone was a penalty rather than a reward. He was not a solitary. So to Andy would come the call, "Whaddaya say we hit a few taverns?" The call of the wild as crooned in Olde Brooklyn.

The taverns were more conversation sites, more scenes of banter and raillery than riotous times. The usually bumptious Jackie often interspersed recollections of youthful hijinks with grim thoughts about how "the college boys [CBS executives] with all their money and limousines have contempt for you and me." The college boys "don't know anything, they know half what we know. They achieved it the easy way. I came up the hard way." The merry man held deep and dour notions of the accepted elite greatly unlike the genial gaiety he normally displayed with the brass. Yet when Bill Paley signed him for thirty-nine weeks at $6 million, the street kid in Jackie requested, "You got any booze around?"

I've known certain actors talented or lucky enough to have climbed from poverty to wealth with a first contract and to have gained landed estate, a patronizing air toward humanity, and a British accent slumbering in their larynx, which heretofore had spoken pure Bronx. Jackie was a boy you could take out of Bushwick, but you could never take the Bushwick out of the boy.

He was a democrat with a small *d* all his days. A Jackie Gleason Company of Players had no captains or corporals— just professionals. Sometimes he went to extremes to make it clear that we were all in this thing together, with no badges of rank.

There was the ultra-ultra dinner party for the more ballistic big-shot executives of the network, sponsors, et cetera, laid on by Mr. Gleason at his personal apartment. The meal was an epicurean adventure, the wines a delicate distinction to every course—all served with aplomb by Jackie's houseman. The guests were overwhelmed but also aware that there was a vacant place at the table. Someone had chosen not to be among the select. Not to worry.

After serving the last visible greats, Jackie's houseman, bringing his plate, pulled up the empty chair and ate and drank his own homemade fare with zest and gusto as his boss smiled appreciatively.

But the simple honesty and the neighborhood loyalty of Jackie was shown in the development of *Gigot*, the movie in which he starred as the poor Parisian deaf-mute. It was Jackie's idea, and he wanted to play the role in a major motion picture. But to sell the story, he would need a professional screen treatment to peddle in Hollywood for financing. He asked Andy to write the treatment, assuring him they would get $50,000 for it and split the money fifty-fifty.

Andy wrote the treatment, wryly noting that he didn't have to write lines for the Gleason part since he was a mute. Jackie flew west to scale the ramparts of Filmdom. Time passed. No word was heard.

Then one morning at 3:00 A.M., Andy's phone rang.

Jackie: "Get up and have a drink, kid. I got news for you."

The news was good and the news was bad. Yes, he had sold Andy's screen treatment but for only $25,000 instead of the $50,000 they were to split.

But to a Brooklyn street kid, a bargain is a vow. "You take all of it. I promised you," said Jackie, and that was it. The Yiddish word *mensch* was known to every New Yorker as defining an honorable man, someone of consequence, of dignity, of character. Andy Russell realized his boss and friend was all of those good things, he said: "How can you fault a guy like that?" It's a matter of style, a case of class. A mensch has to do what a mensch has to do

Audrey Meadows

According to Andy, Jackie was two people—generous, gentle, true, and also a boy of the streets, rough, bitter, harsh. You saw the one he wanted you to see when he wanted you to see it. We never leave our roots. We just grow new branches. Jackie's branches sprouted flowers for the whole world to see, but there were deep thorns too.

★ SNAPSHOT ★

Cleavage, in addition to being the way rocks and ores are naturally split, came to have another meaning in fifties television to which it still refers, i.e., the manner and depth of the division in a woman's dress which displays rocks and ores to greatest danger of lumbar pneumonia. The network execs thought that the black and white screen would turn American males rabid and send them howling into the night.

We didn't have any cleavage problems with the regular players on the Gleason show since Trixie and Alice never got out of bargain basement housedresses and the June Taylor Dancers had to jump and twist and whirl and kick. Dancers exercise very hard, and they certainly want to be sure that all important body parts stay within their clothing. However, our guest stars could and did have minds of their own.

Hollywood actress Terry Moore appeared with Robert Wagner on one of our earlier shows to publicize their new movie, *Beneath the Twelve-Mile Reef*. I was asked if I would let her share my dressing room. Terry and her mother arrived. She was obviously a dedicated stage mother, because she was loaded down with camera equipment, looking like a Japanese tourist.

Terry wore a lovely cocktail dress, but when I saw the neckline I knew trouble was ahead. It went way too far south for CBS. I suggested meekly that wardrobe would undoubtedly want to place a large flower in the center of the décolletage.

If Terry was upset about how silly she would look, her mother was completely undone. Seems she wanted Terry in her full natural bloom, not with any blooming flower. What to do? We yanked the dress up over her lovely attributes and, with the addition of a scarf, the problem was solved. Sorry, guys, blame that stuffy censor. He hated surprises.

Abbe Lane (then Mrs. Xavier Cugat) was famed for her warm delivery and stunning stature, but when she was on our show, she'd also gone skimpy on fabric in the cleavage area. Abbe had a gorgeous figure (and she still does), but the censor decreed and the wardrobe mistress applied a swath of material to disguise salient views of much more of Abbe. Not trusting herself to speak, Abbe minded a temper unrenowned for serenity. Came her entrance cue, and she made a grandiose lunge onto the stage to yells and applause. Her fingers found the offending bit of material, and it negligently floated over her shoulder and away.

Censors are energetic and righteous people, but they just couldn't work a room like Abbe Lane.

★ SNAPSHOT ★

Jackie was fascinated with many aspects of parapsychology and read widely about the subject. He was particularly interested in the many reports of how hypnotism had, presumably, been effective in bringing about medical cures. Somehow he became certain that he himself possessed the skills of a hypnotist. How he reached this judgment, I have no idea, but he never convinced the rest of us.

Novelist and screenwriter Budd Schulberg, a great writer who was also, unfortunately, a habitual stutterer, visited Jackie's apartment to discuss writing some special material for the show. Jackie saw this impediment as a great opportunity for healing through hypnotism. With Budd's permission, Jackie soothed his first patient with mesmerizing eye and dominating voice for a full hour.

Finally, Budd exited Herr Doktor's office, and the production gang pounced on him. "Did Jackie help cure your stuttering?" he was asked.

The author drew himself up, gazed meaningfully at the group with a slow smile, and answered, "D . . . D . . . D . . . Definitely."

And Awaaay We Go

The *Jackie Gleason Show*, in addition to being home for "The Honeymooners," used guest stars. Jackie sought to get the best talent—Peggy Lee, Louis Armstrong, Nat "King" Cole, and many others, and to discover new stars.

I well recall when Jackie had booked a very young southern boy named Elvis Presley, who was a down-home guitar plucker but had a way with a song between a wail and a whisper. I was sitting in the audience with his manager, the good ole boy, self-styled Colonel Parker. Jackie was watching carefully on the monitor and asked for a couple of repeats of the number, intent upon how to photograph Elvis from the waist up, since his lower-body moves would surely not pass the censor. Then Jackie asked for another repeat, and the kid turned sulky, twisting and turning, head down just like a stubborn child who is not going to do what an adult asks him to do. Jackie was patient, but that wouldn't last long, I knew. Here he was giving this unknown the break of his life and the kid was showing him a take-it-or-leave-it tantrum. Elvis was going to be watching the show from his hotel TV unless things changed fast and soon.

Colonel Parker shrugged his jacket wide beside me and sneaked a hand into the inside pocket. He patted his pocket and said, "One more time, Elvis, and I'll give you this." I was fascinated by what he could possibly have in his pocket. Sure enough, the kid's right hand strummed a chord and slid into the intro. He was off on whatever the song was, and tension left the hall. Then, watching closely, I saw Colonel Parker walk to the stage and reward Elvis with a candy bar.

Later, the world learned to wear blue suede shoes.

So, my dears, the King of Graceland, who could have bought the state of Tennessee from petty cash, possessed of more platinum and gold records than a hound dog has ticks, got his first TV network gig with the aid of a candy bar. Ed Sullivan got him second. They must have stocked up on giant Mr. Goodbars.

According to Phil Cuoco, our scenic designer, Colonel Parker met with Jackie later and offered him 50 percent of Elvis for $25,000. Jackie, disgusted with the guitar player's antics, declined with some frankness. Quoted Phil, "Who wants that shimmying son of a bitch?" Lots of people did, Jackie.

Jane Russell, famed more for her chesty still shots than for her acting until she sang, danced, and cracked wise in *Gentlemen Prefer Blondes* and *The French Line* in the fifties, was another Gleason guest star and a sharp and nice lady.

I forget the sketch she was going to be in because I wasn't part of it. I was involved in other things. As her entrance cue approached, Jane did not. Floor managers madly signaled "stretch" to the actors while production assistant Joan Reichman galloped up the stairs and hurled herself into Miss Russell's dressing room to find her, as Joan would report later, "sitting there with no clothes on." The report of such a secondhand vision both stunned and electrified our backstage crew.

It developed that there was more of Jane than there was of dress in the bosom area, and the back zipper refused to go all the way up and lock. To have presented herself in a garment whose unlocked zipper was persistently presenting herself even more to a startled general public would have assured replacement of *The Jackie Gleason Show* with a test pattern.

Squeezing Jane into a somewhat closed dress, Joan bundled her down to the stage after anxious words to the crew. For as the bountiful, if apprehensive, Miss Russell made her entrance, a dwarfish Miss Reichman stumped in her wake on aching knees, holding the inconstant zipper closed with both hands. All cameras panned up as the actors walked into Miss Russell's shot to block the kneeling Joan. Of course, Jane had to move occasionally, as the script action dictated, and the Toulouse Lautrec attendance of Joan came close to demolishing the actors in gulped giggles.

Finally, it was over. Jane remained clothed. Joan had holes in her hosiery. The producer bought the first round. And more.

Shooting live television—the medium's so-called Golden Age—was more difficult for the technicians than it was for the actors. Most of us had experience on Broadway, where, of course, everything is live. On TV, however, there were no lengthy rehearsals, no out-of-town tryouts. None. The show was a one-performance run and you were out looking for a part again. Camera, sound, lighting, and directors were all learning the trade and, oddly enough, so were the on-camera advertising spokesmen, many of whom had been doing network radio for years. We had two lulus whom Joan Reichman found impossible to forget, no matter how hard, as production assistant, she may have tried.

A lissome model, tabbed by someone to extol beauty products, had charmed the guys at the ad agency with her voice and manner. However, she misplaced all her assurance when it suddenly hit her that she had to sell this product to millions and millions of people who might not want to buy it. And there were no retakes. She slipped away to the Cordial Bar, out front of the theatre, and began to talk to the glass, as the saying goes, about her problem. Before the Cordial had to send out for more gin to restore her composure, she made it onstage, hit her mark, smiled, and went into her spiel while in combat with gravity, which endangered the standing set, our contract with the sponsor, and innocent bystanders.

Our ever-vigilant associate producer, Stanley Poss, used an arm like an old-fashioned shepherd's crook to snag her, and the ad was abbreviated along with the model. The folks at home must have thought she was doing one of those South American dances New Yorkers were always doing. Anyway, we got no letters.

The account executive for the Schick razor account closely observed every run-through and rehearsal of the Schick Pre-shave Lotion commercial. The company was paying a lot of money for this prime-time full-network exposure on *The Jackie Gleason Show,* and the account executive wanted to be sure that everything went perfectly. No, better than perfectly, because the client was watching.

Love, Alice

The announcer was handsome, seasoned, sober, responsible. He had been right on the money for timing and tempo on every show.

This time he gave his pitch in a resonant, suave, compelling baritone.

And he called the product the "Shit Prick Shave Lotion."

Millions roared. The adman ate his tie. While he was wearing it.

These minor bumps in the road never seemed to affect Jackie's controlled calmness. I must say, I never saw him come unglued at times that I might have if I were the boss. However, according to my buddy Joan Reichman, he could deliver a scathing postmortem to writers and crew in Sunday A.M. reviews of the night before. He was specific and detailed about errors in scripting or stagecraft, and all present were made aware of what was supposed to have happened and did not or happened in unusual ways. You could defend yourself, but "It's not my fault" tends to weaken in repetition. No one ever got fired, or even threatened with firing, but all were made to recall that despite the breezy, even casual style of the performers, this was an engineered and timed entertainment. That breezy style could become a cold wind for them all if the programming and technical execution became sloppy.

Having firmly emplaced bees in bonnets and burrs under saddles, Our Founder would advise Joan to "meet me in the Mermaid Room" (the bar of the Park Sheraton), and Jackie would drown his sorrows or at least immerse his whistle in strong waters while continuing the autopsy to an audience of one.

Our rehearsals gathered odd lots of show folk from the very beginning to schmooze, or kibitz, or guffaw, but also to give us a big hand. It was like having your own cheerleaders at the scrimmage before the Big Game. In addition to assorted comics and pals from other TV and Broadway shows, we also had two perennial guests, one at rehearsal and one most every Saturday night after the show, both of whom were, most certainly, unique—former middleweight boxing champ Rocky Graziano and Bishop Fulton J. Sheen.

I don't know anything about boxing, but I think everyone in the city knew about New York's own Rocky, who came up from the street gangs to become one of the most fearless fighters ever to step into the ring. His fights with Tony Zale were always described as waterfront brawls, with each of them emerging as walking wounded from blizzards of punches. Yet I was surprised to find that such a storied warrior was not much more than my height. I was five foot six and Rocky barely a half inch taller, with the naturally sturdy and agile build of a middleweight. But he had grown bored with giving and absorbing punishment and decided he would become a TV actor. Television critics never could hit as hard as Tony Zale or Ray Robinson. Personally, I always thought it would be a courageous casting director who would tell Rocky he wasn't right for the part.

Maybe Rocky started dropping in on our rehearsals to pick up a few comedy pointers for use in his own aspiring career, but he became "The Honeymooners" ' most faithful fan. He was amazed at the way I memorized a complete one-hour script Friday night while the news was on and doled out lines as required if gaps occurred in the action. Jackie had already given me the nickname The Ropemaker for weaving rescue lines when he gave me the code of rubbing his stomach in a circular movement, which he had translated as "Throw me a lifeline or we'll all sink!" He rarely needed a line, and we never sank.

But Rocky decided I deserved a particular reward, and

from him. In recognition of my ropemaker duties and frequent role of human maypole among the careening actors
in the Kramden apartment, he graciously sliced his nickname to the core and labeled me The Rock. I don't recall too
many people calling me by such a formidable moniker, but
I did thank him for the singular honor. He was always a
gentleman, and few debated the champ when it came to
matters he viewed as important.

Fat Jack Leonard, aka Jack E. Leonard, a wonderful
comic, was another regular. He called me Rock of, as in
Gibraltar. We used to go see him when he was appearing at
Ben Marden's Riviera nightclub. It was across the bridge on
the Jersey side. He had a rapid-fire delivery, and one night
when he drew an uncooperative audience, he finished his
act with "Thank you very much, ladies and gentlemen, and
when you go home tonight, I hope the bridge opens down!"
Jackie loved him.

Jackie never called me Rock, but he did start introduc-
ing me to CBS roaming executives and sponsors as Our
Audrey, which I grew to learn was common in Irish families, where few Christian names were given. Joe, Tom, Jim,
John, Bill, Frank would be introduced as Our Joe, Our Tom,
and so on, to differentiate them from scores of kids with the
same first names. Rarely would a name like Jason or Lance
or Kirk be heard in Brooklyn. Likewise, Tiffany, Samantha,
and Victoria were definitely non-neighborhood.

I sort of liked Our Audrey—but that was only for company. To the cast and crew, I remained Audrey or Aud.

Bishop Fulton J. Sheen was both a brilliant theologian
and a fascinating speaker who in the fifties had a thirty-
minute prime-time television spot on DuMont called *Life Is
Worth Living*, which was enormously popular. A slender,
handsome man with piercing blue eyes, he did not preach

sectarian creeds nor was he some Bible-banging Billy Sunday type. Instead, he spoke of the vital linkage between a God who was personal to each individual and what that meant in shaping your own life. It wasn't ethereal nor was it pop religion, but its message and its messenger became dear to supposedly tough and cynical New Yorkers. As I recall, he even had a sponsor.

I always supposed that Jackie met the bishop when Jackie was topping *Cavalcade of Stars* at DuMont and that's where their friendship began. All the cast and crew were happy to have him around. I don't recall him ever missing a Saturday night. Jackie and the bishop spent a lot of private time, no doubt discussing Jackie's broken marriage and what, at that time, was called his "fallen away" status in the Catholic Church. The two daughters of the marriage, Geraldine and Linda, lived with their mother. Jackie had been twenty and his wife nineteen when they were married, and I gather from him that things moved from uneasy to brittle to bad and, finally, to bust.

I have no idea why people fall in love, nor, of course, why they fall out of love, and I'm not at all sure that anyone else does. Poets, balladeers, and strolling minstrels have been crooning to the rest of us about true and abiding love for centuries, preferably in words that rhyme, or meters that scan, and they are all full of it.

Passion is great for openers. But in addition to loving that other person, you have to like him/her if you're going to be warming cold feet on each other for years and years. Being gentle and kind and thoughtful is right up there with having eyes like limpid pools (whatever they are) or a firmly jutting chin. The tiny daily joys of a deep love don't fit well into madrigals or sonnets because they're personal to each couple—sweetness, caring, avoiding vulnerabilities, sharing discoveries, gossip, jokes, glad tidings, never going to bed angry at each other. The quiet ardor of matched hearts. If one stumbles, the partner always finds strength enough for two. You grow to become best friends as well as an indivisible couple. For always. It's been happening like this forever, but press on it has been very soft.

When I first worked with Jackie in the boom years of "The Honeymooners," he was going with Marilyn Taylor, June's sister and a dancer with the troupe. Jackie was crazy about Marilyn and I know she cared deeply about him, and not because he was a big star. She cared about the man. Being a good girl, she must have found it very uncomfortable, at times, since although Jackie was separated, he was not divorced. (His wife was not inclined to give him up.) Divorce for Jackie, at the time, was a struggle with his Catholicism. Since I was well aware of their love for each other, I used to talk to him about it. I said, "Jackie, don't you think it's better to live your life in the eyes of God, rather than the church?"

His answer was "Aud, you just don't understand. It's different when you've been raised a poor Irish Catholic from Brooklyn." Marilyn, I imagine, must have decided she could not continue forever this way, so some time later she left the show. She was fortunate enough to marry a wonderful man, make a life in faraway Chicago, and have a son.

Meantime, Jackie rekindled a romance with a former girlfriend, Honey Merrill, a very pretty, sweet blonde. I believe they went together for around fifteen years.

When Jackie was starring on Broadway in *Take Me Along*, he asked me to take Honey to my furrier to buy her a mink coat; then we were to meet him at Sardi's after the matinee.

I said, "Jackie, you mean you trust me to select her mink coat?"

He said, "Sure I do. You know more about these things than I do."

Well, we chose beautiful skins and had her fitted to a muslin pattern so they could make the coat. When we joined him at Sardi's, with Honey still in her wool coat, Jackie's eyes bugged out. "Where's the coat?" he demanded. So we explained that it would be custom made for her and he relaxed.

I don't remember when he and Honey split up, but time passed and Jackie finally got his divorce. Then he met his second wife, Beverly. This was not to be a marriage made in heaven. It lasted about five years. Jackie was then living in Florida, where he was doing his show. Marilyn's husband had passed away, and she went to live in Florida with June. Jackie was separated but not divorced from Beverly, but he was overjoyed to learn Marilyn was back in town. He asked if he could see her.

Marilyn said, "No, not until you're divorced." She certainly didn't make it easy for him. Finally, they were back together where they belonged, married, and she gave him twelve of the happiest years of his life. I was almost as thrilled as they were, because Jackie deserved a wonderful wife and partner and all the joy that she brought him.

★ SNAPSHOT ★

In no particular order, here are some items about Jackie and/or the show that don't have any special place in this saga but that fans of "The Honeymooners" might find interesting:

★ Jackie must have had the biggest florist's bill in New York. Each performance, every woman appearing in the show got a dozen roses from him.

★ I always played Alice wearing flats, since I was five foot six and Jackie was about five nine—I wanted to appear shorter, and, of course, he made me look even thinner than I was.

★ Orson Welles was the originator of the title the Great One for Jackie, and, I must say, Jackie wasn't bashful about using it himself now and then. None of the rest of the gang ever called him anything but Jackie, though, and any fawning toady who called him the Great One was judged a kissup of limited talent and tenure and consigned to Outer Darkness.

★ Jackie's office desk bore a nameplate solemnly reading, "Two elephants are better than one." Go figure.

★ Ralph and Alice frequently kissed off target, despite all those tender hugs. As we pivoted away from the camera, we would give the appearance of a big smooch, but sometimes he'd miss and get my chin, nose, or jaw. A marksman he wasn't. None of the open mouth, exchanging tonsils you see today. We always giggled when he missed.

★ Art Carney's Ed Norton wasn't originally written as a sewer worker. One of the writers tossed the job into a script, and it became a memorable part of the role.

Leonard Stern said he believed that most of Art Carney's physical "shtick" was a parody of his father's mannerisms. When he extended his arms and uncurled his fingers, this was the equivalent of his father shooting his celluloid cuffs. (It wasn't uncommon for people of limited means to wear just shirtfronts and cuffs. To make the cuffs extend beyond their jacket sleeves, they would thrust their arms forward, "shooting the cuffs.")

Art explained that his elaborate hand gestures, which he performed almost every show, before picking up a check, signing his name, playing the piano, and so on, mirrored his father's physical manifestations of reluctance to sign one of Art's bad report cards.

★ When asked where he had come up with the character of Ralph Kramden, the hapless yet not hopeless Bensonhurst bus driver always shooting for the moon and rarely hitting even important parts of the sky, Jackie usually replied, "In my part of Brooklyn, we had a million Ralph Kramdens."

He once told me that the creation of a character "starts with looking at all the people on the subway, figuring out how they might have got that way."

★ Jackie never mentioned the switch of Chauncey Street from Bushwick to Bensonhurst, but it might have been because the area had so descended into the pits economically that no middle-class bus driver's family would live there. In 1950s Bushwick, if you were wearing ears, you were from out of town.

★ *The Honeymooners* cycle that people have been watching for almost forty years is the thirty-nine episodes we shot in 1955–56. In addition to being work which was well received when first shown, I think it preserves a kind of currency, because there are few or no references to events of the period.

★ The biggest laugh Jackie ever got on the show was one he hadn't planned. As I recall, it was a racetrack scene. He had done a quick costume change, which was incomplete: his fly remained ajar. No matter what he said—

straight lines, punch lines, throwaways—the audience fell apart howling with laughter. His shorts were decorated with miniature hearts to make the whole event classic. Jackie found the audience of his dreams. Everything he did was funny—even when he wasn't doing anything. Art finally blocked him out and put him wise. He made repairs instantly, and they finished the scene with the audience still laughing at what had gone before. Someone suggested he keep it in as a standard bit of business. Like Queen Victoria, he was not amused.

★ Jackie told me the character of superswank Reggie Van Gleason was inspired by a patronizing mean drunk at the "21" Club who had not only been obnoxious to Jackie for no reason but also told him that he was ready to punch his lights out if he was man enough to stand up to him. Jackie, veteran of many slugfests as emcee at the old Bucket of Blood saloon in Newark (many years and pounds ago), piled into a cab with the challenger and selected Central Park as an arena. Jackie, jigging feet and flicking fists, was working himself into a prebattle sweat. He threw one punch, causing the well-boiled swell to whine, "Not so fast," and wander off into the park shrubbery to insult a couple of trees, who would not become violent. With a few nips and tucks, Jackie created Reggie Van Gleason, the toff's toff, and years of comic scripts.

Love, Alice

★ Jackie was personally one of the worst automobile drivers in America, and the thought of his being a professional bus driver was an inside joke for the whole cast. He wasn't reckless, he was just inept! (True stories in Chapter Eleven.)

★ Art was a good driver but a poor navigator. He'd give Val, my manager, and me a lift home following every show. After dropping me off in Manhattan, he'd deliver Val to his home in the Bronx, then head for his own wife and family in Yonkers. But every Saturday night he got lost. He'd somehow take a wrong turn and find himself on the George Washington Bridge going to New Jersey. The toll booth attendants got to know him well, coming and going.

"I'm sure they think I'm smuggling something," Art surmised.

Marilyn Monroe Never Lived on Chauncey Street

It was Jackie's fortieth birthday—a momentous event in any man's life. Toots Shor had turned over the large upstairs room of his establishment for a party to mark the joyous occasion. Bartenders industriously poured and poured and poured the night away, while busy waiters presided over groaning boards of Shor's version of delicacies and delights on wooden trestles covered by tablecloths. Celebrity counters could be sure that everyone who was anyone was there. And then it was everyone plus two.

Marilyn Monroe and Joe DiMaggio joined the gala.

Marilyn possessed the magical gift of transforming all men into Irish setters who, upon seeing her, frolicked about for no sensible reason, pawed the floor, and smiled many teeth. They fawned in such an absurd manner that you were sure they wanted to be scratched behind the ears. Their tongues didn't exactly loll from gaping mouths, but they came close as they fixated on her every aspirated word.

Despite the fact that a Monroe entrance had the effect of transforming every other woman in the place into a soft boy, we women liked her too. She was the ultimate Homecoming Queen, sensuously bathing in the tidal waves of affection, nay, idolatry, while not trying to put her brand on any of the mouth breathers who had come to do her homage. Marilyn Monroe was a sterling silver star, whose real acting ability was often obscured by her physical attributes. She knew she was a star, and we knew, and she played the role from first loge to last balcony. It was a drama lesson just to watch her shine.

As the male population of North America surrounded her, babbling incoherently, wise women refusing to converse with bowls of potato salad or bartenders who wanted to talk with Joltin' Joe, sought that sacred haven of the ladies' room. I was of that number.

Presumably, when large numbers of ladies had retired to their room, one of the lusty gallants attempted to lift Mrs. DiMaggio onto one of the impromptu trestle tables, rich in cholesterol, for a photo. But either the lifter had left his muscles on the squash court or the lady was more solid than dainty porcelain, because the hoist was less than successful. No, the table didn't break nor did the food become airborne, but Marilyn learned that it was important for her, too, to leave center stage and visit the ladies' room.

As I recall, there were three of us before the vanity mirrors, assisting nature with puff and lipstick, when she entered our new home away from home—Jean Carney, Art's wife; Rosemary Wilson, columnist Earl Wilson's B.W. (Beautiful Wife); and yours truly. However, when I've recounted this tale, other women recall they were also present. If all are right, Shor's ladies' room must have been nearly as big as DiMaggio's Yankee Stadium, but, hey, I didn't take roll call.

Marilyn swept in wearing that molded-to-the-body black dress with spaghetti shoulder straps, and she looked most fetching, but she had a problem.

In that wispy little girl voice, she exhaled, "Ladies, I wonder if you can help me. I seem to have gotten a splinter in my ass."

Proving her point, she upped her skirt, and I will give testimony that she certainly did have a splinter in her ass.

But Jean Carney, an experienced mother familiar with splinter crises, acted with aplomb. A straight pin, sterilized by my cigarette lighter's flame, and Doctor Carney probed and produced with a technique Johns Hopkins couldn't have matched. And she waived her fee. Marilyn was most grateful.

When we told Jackie, he reported that his carnation pin was carefully honed for just such emergencies, and we should please keep him in mind for the next surgical procedure. Especially if Marilyn was afflicted again.

I got to know Marilyn Monroe fairly well because we shared the same dressmaker in New York. He was an inspired designer and a superb finisher, but there was one problem—Marilyn.

The dressmaker would always be very late for my appointment if he had a prior one with Marilyn. Thirty minutes, forty, an hour he'd be perched in an anteroom of her apartment awaiting the Monroe presence. She was not just tardy. She was unreachable until her personal clock struck.

What was more important to her? She had moved her bed over to the window. She would be lying on it munching ripe, red apples while observing the chaos of Manhattan traffic from her private perch as a form of entertainment.

The designer was hesitant to complain, but I was not. I

told her, in spirited tones, that when she kept him waiting, she was keeping me waiting. She was apologetic in her kittenish way, and promised to be good in that breathy child's voice, so we switched to grown-up girl talk about gossip, movies, men, and other vital concerns.

But nobody could persuade Marilyn to do anything on time. Vexed, I mentioned the problem to Jackie. "Take away her apples," he advised. "Tell her they'll make her lumpy." Yet Marilyn was not about to become lumpy. She was pledged to retain her most prominent physical attributes. She had a special routine for a thorough thoracic workout.

Kidnapping our designer and his buddy, my hairdresser, she took them to Central Park Lake for a brisk two hours of rowboat voyaging. While she wore sunglasses and a black wig as a disguise, she insisted one of the guys don a flowing blond wig. Marilyn was to be the rowboat's one-man crew, and the boy-girl passengers sat in the back as ballast. Up the lake, down the lake, around the lake they toured as Marilyn heaved and stretched strong arms to encourage surprised muscles and tendons to make firm the Monroe chest.

When Jackie was told about this singular water sport, I steeled myself for a superbawdy response. But the very picture of this endeavor to maintain and enhance two of the great wonders of the modern world had stunned him into a state approaching awe.

"If she'll let me ride in her rowboat," he said in a solemn prayer, "I'll buy her a battleship." And he added, "I'll even wear that wig."

Around this time I had such a nice woman working for me part-time, cleaning the apartment and taking care of my clothes. (We'll call her Bridey.) One day Bridey came to me and with much hemming and hawing asked for a favor. She said a woman she had worked for in the past was back in town and needed her again. Bridey said, "It won't interfere with your job because she gets up very early and I want to get there before she orders the groceries. Then I'll come to you, and when I finish here, go back to her place to cook dinner." When I asked who the lady was, she said she'd rather not say. My interest piqued by this mysterious person, I asked, "Why do you have to order the groceries?"

"Because if I don't get there before the stores open, she will have ordered six gallons of milk, four dozen eggs, a fourteen-pound turkey, a sixteen-pound roast beef, and a leg of lamb, plus so many vegetables that I can't fit them all in her refrigerator."

A light went on inside my head, and I said, "Is the lady Marilyn Monroe?" When she said yes, I naturally told her, "Of course, you can go help her out." I was dying to know what Marilyn was doing with all that food. A few days later, I said, "Bridey, does Miss Monroe entertain a lot?" "No, not really" came her answer, "but she will have two or three friends over. She'll ask me to cook a turkey and a leg of lamb and all the fixin's despite my telling her it's too much for three people. Then, when dinner is over, she will come into the kitchen and say, 'Bridey, would you mind if I gave the turkey to Susie and the lamb to my other friend to take home?' "

I was touched to learn this side of Marilyn. All of her success and abundance could not erase the abandoned little girl inside. Food was important to a kid who grew up in foster homes. It was so prized, it made the perfect gift.

For the reader's Unsolved Mystery File, I submit a small enigma. When I went to CBS's photo department in New

York to get pictures of all of us on the show, I also asked for Marilyn Monroe's file to see if there were any of her at Gleason's party at Toots Shor's that I didn't have. I was told by Marty Silverstein, the very able head of the department, that all the pictures in her file had strangely disappeared several years ago. I was lucky enough to have the one you see in this book as a longtime souvenir.

With all the pictures of Marilyn in print, why would someone, or someones, have been so eager to grab the entire photo file of Marilyn at CBS?

Who knows, and, you may well say, who cares? Well, I find it peculiar. Is this a groupie of enormous proportion, or what?

As they say—the plot thins.

How Sweet It Is

Playing the Palace used to be the top for vaudeville performers. In the forties and fifties, ever since Frank Sinatra had turned it into a pandemonium of screaming bobby-soxers, the Paramount Theatre was the equivalent of the Palace Theatre on Broadway. As at Radio City, live performers shared the bill with feature films. And with the success of "The Honeymooners" on television, someone had the idea of putting Kramden & Co. on the stage—and so we found ourselves topping the bill at the Paramount for a two-week stint. Seven days a week, six shows a day, and we still had to do our TV show Saturday night.

Never having played a movie theatre before, I had no idea what it entailed. We started very early in the morning. Audiences were in there at 9:00 A.M. I wondered if they were out of work, skipping school, or what.

You'd think a two-hour movie would give you plenty of

time between shows—it doesn't. You come off the stage, take the elevator to your dressing room, have something to eat, make a phone call, freshen your makeup, then back in the elevator down to the stage again. We worked so late that there wasn't really time to go home. So most of us stayed at the Astor Hotel across the street so we could get some sleep.

The hotel being so fully booked, we couldn't get a room for my theatre maid, who lived way uptown. I knew she'd be a basket case if she had to commute, and since I had twin beds, I said she could stay with me. Big mistake!

I always read at night, but she conked off as soon as her head hit the pillow. A few minutes later the thunderstorm hit—I have never heard anyone snore like that in my life. Toying with the idea of returning to my apartment, I mentioned my problem to Jack Philbin the next day.

"Don't you know how to stop someone from snoring?" he asked.

"If I did, I would have."

"All you have to do," Philbin explained, "is whistle a high, sustained whistle a time or two, and they stop right away." That night I felt like an idiot sitting in bed whistling, but it worked. A couple of harumph, harumps and it stopped. How's that for a helpful hint?

Back to the Paramount. Fortunately, we did the same sketch for all six shows, but Saturday we had a logistical problem—how to get to Studio 50 for rehearsal, back to the Paramount for the stage show, then back to Studio 50 for *The Jackie Gleason Show* from 8:00 to 9:00, where we were doing a different script, then back to the Paramount again. It was solved with a siren-blaring police escort, which just managed to get us to both places in time.

"The Honeymooners" script prepared by Leonard Stern and Syd Zelinka for this Saturday's show was to be one of our funnicst. But Jackie called them late Friday afternoon to say that the script didn't work. He wanted them to come to the theatre. Leonard said they couldn't come immediately. Jackie was adamant that they meet, and the only way to meet was after our last show at 11:30 P.M. Leonard left a message for Syd to meet him in the drugstore of Jackie's hotel—there was a crisis.

When he arrived at the drugstore, there was a nervous Syd surrounded by ten spouses of production personnel. Jackie had summoned almost everybody involved in the show for the conference. Reluctantly, they went upstairs to Gleason Enterprises.

The first thing to greet them was a roomful of drunks. There wasn't a sober soul on a single sofa. It was understandable. They'd been waiting and drinking for hours. Jackie came out of the bedroom, grunted a "hello," and told them the script did not make any sense. As proof, he cited many lines which to him were baffling. In a flash, they realized what had happened. In those days, a script page was divided in half—dialogue on the right, stage directions on the left. This show, a spoof on *Beat the Clock*, the CBS show which preceded us on Saturday nights, was more physical than any show they had done up to that time. Seventy-five percent of the lines referred to the actions depicted in the stage directions, and Jackie had ignored the directions.

Eating crow, he told them he would do the show, but cautioned Leonard and Syd, "Don't say anything to them," indicating the inebriates.

Ralph and Alice had appeared as contestants on *Beat the Clock*, running out of time before completing the next stunt. The emcee, Bud Collyer, asked the Kramdens to return the following week. The next scene opens in the kitchen about

2:00 A.M., with Ralph, Alice, and Ed practicing the stunt so we'll win. One of us has to pick up a cup from a table, the other grab the saucer, put the cup on the saucer, and get to the lemon machine before the lemon comes down and falls on the floor, keeping a balloon in the air the whole time. Ed is playing the lemon machine, and broken dishes are all over the floor when Alice has a speech explaining how we should do it without bumping into each other.

I started to talk and heard myself go so tongue-twisted it made no sense. Jackie and Art stared at me deadpan.

I stamped my foot and said, "See, you've got me so nervous I can't talk straight. Now I'm going to say it over till I get it right." Which I did very slowly.

When I finished, Jackie gave me a look and said, "Big deal!" and the audience howled.

On the way back to the Paramount in the police car, Jackie was so tickled. "Aud, Aud, if you could have seen your face, it was so funny when you got mad." He loved it. Today, of course, if you foul up they do another take.

It was a two-week gig at the Paramount, and doing the same show six times a day gets you into the sillies. I never ever broke up on "The Honeymooners," no matter how funny the script. It was funny to me, Audrey, when I read it, but it was not funny to Alice. We played truth. But, and a big but—Jackie decided to go after me at the Paramount. He and Art were in on it together.

One show he left the script entirely and made up lines like "Oh, I know about you, Alice. You think I don't. I know about you up on the roof with Polacks." A scream from the balcony.

"And I know all about you and the Chinese waiter in the Hong Kong Gardens." Art stood behind him, making

Norton faces, agreeing. The two of them were so outrageous and funny that I broke and started to laugh. If I'm tired, you better not get me started laughing, because I can't stop. I laughed so hard Jackie turned to the audience and said, "You know what I like about her? When she laughs, her stomach bounces."

That did it. I collapsed onto one of the kitchen chairs, and the chair leg broke, as if on cue, and I descended backward with legs flying in the air. The roar from the theatre audience sounded like Frankie was back in town. That's the only time they ever got me.

When we opened at the Paramount, the line was three deep all the way around the block. Unfortunately, New York City began to drown under a rain reaching for a monsoon toward the end of our second week. The audience was getting down to strong swimmers and tourists trying to find a dry place to sit down.

The weather put gloom on us all, especially Jackie. Val and I were sitting in my dressing room when Jackie's dresser, Eddie Divierno, appeared and asked us to visit with Jackie because he was getting depressed. Val is a very upbeat person and was the perfect companion. So down we went to raise Jackie's spirits. Later, as we left, Jackie commented, "You don't know how lucky you are, Aud. You have Val. All my people have left me."

Toast of New York, top show in the nation, yet all alone on a rainy evening.

Jackie knew literally hundreds of people, but strangely none that I know ever claimed that they shared any special closeness with him. He was bright, engaging, witty, kind, sensitive, reliable—all characteristics you'd select if you were casting perfect friends, but he seemed to be always surrounded by acquaintances, or fellow performers, rather than buddies. Art Carney certainly knew Jackie best, and I can't believe there was ever a harsh word passed between them, yet they led different lives. Jack Haley, Don Ameche, and, of course, Toots Shor were people with whom he had shared many happy times, but his closest friends, of whom Haley was one of the best, lived in California. Milton Berle, Jack E. Leonard, and Phil Silvers were three of his favorite comic sidekicks.

Yet Jackie rarely called others by their given names. It was always "pal" or "pal-o'-mine," and I was never sure whether the man who had a photographic memory used such a greeting as a barrier.

One time Marilyn Taylor called to ask me if I would bring a date and come for dinner at Jackie's apartment. I asked who else would be there, and Marilyn said, "I don't know yet—I just want Jackie to have more friends."

For all his vivacity, Jackie could seem hesitant in social situations. El Morocco was a Manhattan nightclub which was very fashionable in the days of Café Society, under owner John Perona definitely the in place, with good food and a great band. I used to go dancing at Elmo's almost every night. Very often John would invite me and my date to sit at his table, where he used to entertain the international set and close friends.

John was a big fan of Jackie's and kept asking me why he didn't come in. When I relayed this to Jackie, I was surprised to get his almost plaintive reply, "How do I know I'll get a good table?"

He didn't realize the power of his success would open doors for him everywhere.

"Jackie, John will give you the best table in the house, he'll be so delighted."

"Okay, Aud, you make the reservation, and we'll go."

Love, Alice

There was a house rule at El Morocco and the "21" Club that no customers could approach celebrities and bother them. Consequently, famous people or stars frequented both establishments. Marilyn, Jackie, and I went one night after the show. John was thrilled and made a big fuss over Jackie. Many drinks later, Jackie was getting sleepy, and his head began to nod on his chest. I heard a voice say, "Good evening, Mr. Gleason," and looked up to see Bill Paley entering with his wife. The most amazing transformation took place. Jackie sat up wide awake and cold sober to exchange pleasantries with him.

Enough about this seemingly vacant area of Jackie's life. He was a man who could be uncomfortable by himself, but he was not a desperately lonely guy, if this makes any sense. He consumed books on every phase of life and remembered everything. While none of us knew it at the time, he obviously was hearing magnificent music in his head, which in one of the magical achievements of his life he would compose. He would lead great orchestras in producing spectacular recordings of romantic mood music which were not only enchanting but enormously successful. Such unexpected talent was more than flair. A complex man, Jackie lived in a complex inner life.

As I mentioned, he used to discuss his marital problems with me as a friendly and confidential ear more than as a counselor, I'm sure. I think I can sum up our conversations by saying that Jackie was a family man in search of a family. He could have been a model father figure if his home life had been more stable. He adored his two daughters. What he told me, and how he told me, remains personal, even though he is no longer here to care about his privacy. I am here and I do care.

Whatever his personal concerns, and they reached deep within him, Jackie never wore a long face, never let private woe become public mood. He would greet all the company with winks and smiles, a peppery badinage, an arch comment about network hierarchy, an unbarbed arrow at an inflated target.

Aside from the gags and put-ons, he could amaze you with a sudden intuitive touch. Jackie was unaware my father had suffered a serious stroke. I had told no one. I don't believe in carrying private problems to work; we carry enough baggage with us as it is. During a rehearsal, as I was crossing the stage, he sensed something and said to me, "I don't know what it is, Aud, but if it's anything I can help you with, I'm here."

Today, forty years after the Golden Years of *The Honeymooners* and *The Jackie Gleason Show*, young people who see Jackie on our eternal reruns ask the perennial question, "What was he like?"

I feel they're disappointed with my answers, which are usually too broad in their brevity. "Buoyant." "Playful." "Loyal." "Marvelous." All of the above. He also possessed the ability to dominate a room when he entered it just by his presence. Jackie never had any retinue to praise the king. He just became a focus, a large, smiling, good-looking man, always well-dressed and impeccably groomed, radiating a warmth. People edged closer to the glow.

Known as one of the most amiable men in Show Business, Jackie was popular with the bosses and the bossed, i.e., the rest of us. Yet one Saturday, as rehearsals began, he suddenly became upset with the way the script was playing and let loose with a little profanity.

Our director, Frank Satenstein, cautioned Jackie over the intercom system to watch his language. "Von Faulkenburg is watching." Jackie learned at that moment for the first time that his rehearsals were being monitored by CBS Vice President Von Faulkenburg on a closed-circuit TV in his home in the country for the amusement of his friends and family. Treating performers like dancing bears for the pleasure of the gentry had enraged our Jackie. He took center stage, announced to Mr. Von Faulkenburg and every member of the company, "No show tonight," and walked off.

He got to me as he did to Art and Joyce before we reached our dressing rooms. "Just stay put," he directed. "Don't go home! I'll work this out. DON'T TELL ANYONE that we're going to do the show!" Unbeknownst to me, Jackie had called Leonard and Syd earlier to come down to the theatre immediately and rewrite a scene, which they did.

Five pages later they came down to the stage to find a dark theatre and everybody gone. This was the Twilight Zone—for real. Desperately searching for signs of life, Syd and Leonard dashed to a nearby bar, where some of the cast and crew were congregated. There they learned what had happened.

It seems that when Mr. Big's TV set gave him a marvelous view of an empty studio, his assistant Mr. Big, from Manhattan, called him. His first word was *"Help!"* He was aware that his afternoon entertainment wasn't going to live up to expectations. And if Gleason actually sat out the evening show, Bill Paley would make certain that many executive offices would be vacated by Monday morning.

Through couriers unknown, Jackie was assured that the only reason such a home viewing was arranged was because Mrs. Big was quite ill and (for vague and unrecorded reasons) couldn't see the show at its regular time.

Jackie, always the sentimentalist, growled, "Well, no one told me that."

He let them sweat till after 6:00 P.M. By 6:30 all the

proper concessions, promises, and genuflections had been made for Jackie to return to the theatre. By 7:00 P.M. everybody was back and ready to perform. There was, however, one remaining problem: five new pages of script that had to be given to four different actors and only one copy. There were no duplicating machines in those days. There was an immediate recruitment. Anyone who could type—secretaries, showgirls, stagehands—was given pages to type.

At a quarter to eight, fifteen minutes before the show, five scripts. In those fifteen minutes, and in between scenes, Jackie, Art, and I and the two character people learned our lines and went on. Miracle of miracles, the scene worked.

But no one at the network ever poked the bear in the ribs with a stick again.

★ SNAPSHOT ★

Actor George Petrie, a vital member of Jackie's most informal repertory company of Old Reliables, could play any role the script called for with a voice, manner, and style he invented for the occasion. You call that acting, folks. Jackie liked him a lot and was confident with him in any scene.

The only stage direction Jackie ever gave him, George said, was: "If you want to stay in the picture, stay close to me."

The rest of the cast remembered a television director's adage. It was the command to Cameras 1, 2, and 3: "Follow the money."

And we know who "The Money" was, don't we?

George had some lively ideas about Ralph Kramden and Ed Norton and their relationship to the audience.

Ralph Kramden was a loser. Ed Norton was runner-up, George thought. More people identify with losers than with winners because there's a lot more on the nonwinning side. People laughed at Ralph and Ed, but when plotlines turned emotional, sentimental, the audience responded to the mood. They weren't impatient for the boys to turn into cartoons again. They awarded sympathy, gave compassion.

Because deep down they had found parts of themselves in the characters.

You said it, George. . . .

Frank Marth also played many characters with us, and like George Petrie, he was worth his weight in gold. He had started with Jackie on *Cavalcade* as a very young actor. Joe Cates, the producer, had called him to do a small part in a jail scene titled "The Last Mile and a Half." He and Art were the two prisoners in the sketch. When Jackie got his big contract at CBS and was putting together what turned out to be almost a stock company of players, he remembered Frank and said, "Get me that kid who played the jail sketch." Jackie had a keen eye for talent, and like an elephant he never forgot. And, he was always right on the mark.

I asked Frank what he remembered most about working with Jackie. He said, "Apart from the fact that he always called me Francis, I always felt like I was going to a party, instead of work. It was such a blast."

★ SNAPSHOT ★

Comic actors very probably have one or more screws loose or they would have gone straight and got a clean-hands job at the factory—any factory. Such consideration is prompted by the irrelevant behavior with which actors entertain themselves when they are not entertaining you. This bizarre conduct is neither sophisticated nor even adult. Zany and irrational are the best modifiers.

When Art was driving Val and me home every Saturday night after the show, we had a tendency to make the trip through Manhattan streets a remembrance of the high school bus after the Big Game, with passengers hooting at pedestrians in the smart-aleck caterwauling of unconstrained teenagers letting off noisy steam or triumphant spirits. That was us.

A swiftly walking musician with a violin case would be razzed, "I told you that you gotta get a better finish to the act!" Bawled by loud malcontents.

A lady wheeling a baby carriage would be cautioned by Val with "Don't blame me, I live in Wilkes-Barre."

Why do I abruptly have the feeling I just blew my image as a cool, statuesque, urbane woman of subtle charm and veiled mystery?

And so she continues. If you're going to make a damn fool of yourself, go all the way. . . .

At Jackie's place in Lauderhill, Florida, we broke up script reading with nonsense games in the lounge (read: bar). Give the initials of a star and the other idlers and layabouts had to guess the actor or actress. We got tired of asking, "alive or dead," so for "dead" we substituted "took a cab." Art irreverently said, "When Jackie goes, he'll take a bus." When we got through separating the sheep from the goats of the known world, we descended into touchy-feely games which really would have knocked out the twelve-year-olds at summer camp. Closing your eyes and touching tongue tips is as erotic as playing giant steps, but we gave that a whirl when all other illogical ideas for games for fun and profit had been exhausted. (See pictures with Art starting the game.)

Age had not mellowed such an unruly group, but it certainly had caused harsh trauma to our dignity and deportment.

A Little Traveling Music

There's a lot you can tell by looking at a person. And everyone in the United States in the fifties could tell that Jackie Gleason enjoyed eating. Jackie never claimed gourmet status. He was more of a trencherman.

He enjoyed the taste of food, of course, but he also enjoyed it in quantity. Somewhere in the wilds of the Bronx, he had discovered a pizzeria restaurant which produced a pizza of such size, variety, and sheer weight that he often made late-night emergency runs for sustenance, summoning Jack Philbin or Jack Hurdle as companions. In desperation, a few times, he sent Eddie Divierno to the Bronx to rush a Gleason Special right to his dressing room. I will take an oath that it was as big as the top of a card table, and Jackie found it spicy, satisfying, and almost filling. He would offer each of us a slice and finish the rest himself. Joyce and I could hardly finish one slice, especially since I don't like to eat before a show.

When we were in Miami doing a special, I discovered a marvelous seafood restaurant, right near my hotel, which also served immorally scrumptious chocolate cake. I told Jackie how splendidly I had supped the night before. He was practically salivating as I recounted the specials.

He said, "You have a limo, don't you, Aud? Do you think when you go back to the hotel you could take the driver and order dinner for me?"

I said, "Sure, what do you want?"

He said, "Order me four lobsters, six orders of clams casino, six orders of french fries, and I better have a chocolate cake. Oh, and a salad, too."

I said, "For how many people?"

"Just two, my doctor and me."

I asked him if he invited the doctor in order to pump out his stomach between courses. He gave me a patented har-de-har-har and suggested that missionaries' daughters had lived so long among the starving Chinese that all they could eat was rice balls and fortune cookies.

When the limo picked me up the next day, I asked the driver if he had gotten everything delivered all right.

He said, "Boy, Mr. Gleason must have been hungry. He was standing in his robe at the front door waiting for me."

When we played Atlantic City, my husband, Bob Six, an elected member of several celebrated food and wine societies, had discovered a phenomenal Chinese restaurant about half an hour away. So we decided to give a party for the cast. We invited Jackie and a dozen or so players and production members to a memorable feast there. Bob had ordered a sumptuous dinner, and the delighted Cantonese owner promised to keep the kitchen open till we arrived. He was inspired to create incredible culinary monuments for Mr. Gleason's group. Party members soon collapsed with

Love, Alice

distended stomachs and bleary eyes, but Mr. Gleason stead-
fastly didn't let the side down and ate as fast as our chef
could cook. In the A.M., we were all looking for Chinese
Alka-Seltzer except Jackie, who was shoveling in an ample
breakfast.

Back at the Park Sheraton, he was known to order huge
meals for breakfast, especially after he had attempted to
empty the spirits cellars of Toots Shor's, "21," Jimmy Ryan's, and Joe & Rose's in one evening's hard labor. His
defense against a building hangover, which would have
proven lethal to lesser men, was rolls of French bread the
size of footballs, dipped into banquet boats of beef gravy. I
don't know how this warded off awesome pain in head and
organs, but it worked, or Jackie thought it did, which was
just as good. One morning, writer Walter Stone was late for
the Sunday meeting Jackie was organizing in his weakened
condition.

Walter rushed in saying, "Sorry I'm late, but the elevator
was full of gravy bowls." Jackie shook with laughter even
though it hurt.

On another Saturday morning, he phoned me and said,
"I have to see you right away—script trouble. Come right
over." Thoughts of nude floor lamps flitted through my
mind, but, no, he was too smooth to pull that stunt on me
again.

I said, "Jackie, I'm still in bed. I have to shower and get
breakfast."

"Hurry up" was the word from on high. No sooner was
I out of the shower than it was My Master's Voice on the
phone: "Where are you? You can have breakfast over here.
Forget your lipstick. You'll just smear it on my cups."

I arrived to find the pair of Jacks—Philbin and Hurdle,
our producers—on the premises, but no ladies, with or

without lampshades. Tony, Jackie's valet-chef-houseman-friend, rustled up a quick breakfast, but Jackie said, "Take your time, Aud." Worried about the script, I gulped down something and coffee, and met the three of them in the living room.

"What's the problem?"

"I'm holding a contest between the three of you to see who has the best chicken recipe. What's yours, Aud?"

You will note the life of an actress is not exclusively tinsel and tiaras. Sometimes, it's how do you cook chickens, and it's a contest yet. Did Helen Hayes go through this?

A clergyman's daughter knows a lot of chicken recipes, because fowl is cheaper than beef, so I recited one of my thrifty numbers with a catchy title and a garden of spices to confuse the eater. Practically before I finished, Jackie yelled, "You win, Aud."

My tiny thrill at having won something suddenly was touched by that still, small voice which whispered, "Audrey, you have been set up."

I said, "I win what?"

"You get to cook the chickens for the party tonight."

"Wait a minute," I remonstrated. "I don't cook for armies. I cook for six or maybe eight people."

"That's okay, Aud, I won't invite a lot of people. Just tell Tony what to purchase, and he'll take care of everything." Hurdle and Philbin looked relieved, which did not make me relieved, but, the contest having been decided, we all went off to the theatre to do the show.

When I arrived at the apartment later that night, Jackie greeted me at the door with the biggest orchid corsage I've ever seen. It extended from shoulder to knee. Wearing it, I closely resembled a mobile botanical garden. The second presentation was an all-encompassing chef's apron.

"Tony will help," advised Jackie, "and I will greet the guests." Jack Hurdle, who was a good cook, offered to assist, and we went in the kitchen to find forty dismembered chickens—count them, forty—garnished and spiced long enough to resurrect them to barnyard life. Good old Tony hacked veggies into salads, and Jackie ran in occasional drinks to keep the help from turning mutinous. I had told him that one chicken would feed two guests.

"How many people did you ask to drop in?" I asked, in a voice rising in stridency and volume.

"Oh, you know how these things get around," he offered airily.

Time passed. My orchid tree clutched me from shoulder to knee in as sad condition as the late chickens, also victims of being undercooked on demand.

I had started at 10:00 P.M. It was now 2:00 A.M. Dim sounds of revelry echoed back to the kitchen; Tony had wandered off to bar, or to bed. Jackie arrived requesting more chicken for the party going public.

"Jackie," I intoned in a voice more weary than wrathful, "the last chickens are on the stove. They're not thoroughly cooked. They're still pink inside."

"That's okay, Aud." He grinned. "This mob is too bagged to know whether they're eating chicken or tuna fish." Remembering his manners, he said to the cook, "Have you had any?"

"No, thank you," I said. "After four hours with these birds, I feel we've become too close for that."

At the end of the party, Jackie thanked me profusely and announced, "Aud, I almost never, ever make a mistake, and when I hired you, I knew you could cook forty chickens."

Over the years, Jackie requested different recipes from me, and I was always happy to comply. Sometimes his valet would call and say, "Mr. Gleason says you have a great recipe for pork chops, could you give that to me again?" I would recite it, but I made sure I didn't attend the event at which they were to be served. Cook's night out.

Jackie built a home away from home—his house in Peekskill, New York. It was completely round and, presumably, built primarily with parties in mind.

I got my first look at the place when Jackie invited a group of us to come up one Sunday. I was surprised to find that we entered the home on a sweeping, downward ramp. The house was built into the side of a hill and sort of resembled a flying saucer. The expanse of the place was enormous. We crowded about Jackie as he led the tour of the biggest igloo in the USA, including a huge circular shower stall, with showerheads on all three sides, plus top to bottom, to squirt the interior and the person within. The huge TV set hung from the bedroom ceiling.

In every room, Jackie had designed beautiful Italian marble fireplaces that were half inside and half outside the house. Unfortunately, since they were crafted in Italy, he couldn't find workmen in the United States to install them, so he had to import Italians to do the job. They surely ate well while they were doing it, since the owner was never short on groceries.

Somewhere, Jackie had heard that the submarine USS *Nautilus*, which had recently traveled underwater to the North Pole, had the largest jukebox in the world aboard to entertain the crew in their tedious voyage. Somehow, Jackie said he persuaded the Wurlitzer Company to build him an even bigger one. There it was, ready to spin everything from ragtime to classics with a library of records, including his own, naturally.

Love, Alice

On entering this fascinating house, I was staggered by this very large, round room decorated only by a grand piano and minimal furniture. Crossing the exquisite marble floor, I noticed a very small, round hole. I pointed it out to Bullets, gasping, "My God, they've left a hole in this floor! It will have to be fixed."

Bullets laughed and said, "No, it won't. That's in case any of his friends want to sing. Jackie can press a button, and a microphone rises from under the floor, and the singer can go full round-house network with his rendition."

"Of course, how stupid of me. I should have known that."

As might be expected, the star of the show was the bar, which seemed at least thirty to forty feet long. It would take three bartenders to service it. Betcha the submarine's crew would have swapped the second biggest jukebox in the world for the round-house bar.

On the wall at the far end of this room was an almost life-size painting of Jackie in World War I uniform bearing the simple nameplate "Our Founder." Jackie pointed it out, saying, "He's the guy responsible for it all."

Phil Cuoco, who presided over a lot of the alterations to the Peekskill round house, also was dragooned into becoming Jackie's exercise partner there when Jackie sporadically decided to slim down fifty or sixty pounds. Jackie and Phil would get on their marks on a hill just above the house and run madly down it, whereupon Tony would drive their tiny Nash car over to them. Jackie would get in, and Jackie and Tony would drive back up the hill while Phil ran up it. Then the exercise would be repeated until Jackie felt that he had slimmed enough of himself for one morning.

Phil lost five pounds. Jackie gained ten.

Naturally, if you have a completely round house, you have an enormous round bed, right? You couldn't wake up on the wrong side of Jackie's Peekskill bed. There were no sides, just rims of a perfect circle. But, for reasons unknown, he didn't sleep in this jewel of the bedmaker's art. There was a nice, normal house already on the property, and when it came to sleepy time, Bullets said, "Jackie moves from round to square and uses the bedroom of the old house." Why he commuted between houses to sleep remained an unasked question. Could be that waking up in that round job in billows of sheets in the middle of the night made you think you were lost at sea.

For all his wealth, we never thought Jackie took money very seriously. He didn't know a stock from a bond, wasn't into gold futures and oil leases. He was smart enough to learn any money management he could wish, but it just wasn't his style.

A friend of his, Davey Shelley (the stepson of producer and songwriter Buddy DeSylva), told me that he went to see Jackie shortly before the first show of his new contract in 1952. He walked in to find Jackie in his bedroom packing a steamer trunk. On the bed were assorted clothes and on the desk stacks of bills in different denominations. As they chatted, Jackie would roll three or four of the bills into a pair of socks, some underwear, or an old shirt, and cram the bundle deep into the trunk.

"May I ask what you're doing? You should be out celebrating," said the dumbfounded Davey.

"I have been poor before in my life," Jackie told Davey. "Right now, I'm rich. So I'm packing a cash nest egg in this trunk, and I'm sending it to a warehouse with a will call on it in case I ever need it."

You can be sure that trunk is gathering dust somewhere.

★ SNAPSHOT ★

Cary Grant, witty, tanned, tailored, debonair, and altogether gorgeous, met me when I was on the Paramount lot in Hollywood during a "Honeymooners" summer break. "I heard you were on the lot, and I just had to meet you," he greeted. Later, I made a movie with him, *That Touch of Mink*, and we became good friends, but any woman's initial meeting with Cary is right up there with the big moments of her world history. I was unprepared to discover that the most handsome man in the world was not visiting to see me as much as to tell me how much he adored "The Honeymooners," and how he would very much like to play a one-time part in the show.

"Tell Jackie I just have to be in that kitchen with all of you."

Somehow Brooklyn and bus driver and the Kramden apartment didn't mesh gears in my fuddled brain with the man who had given millions of women delightful heart pangs for years.

"I could be Ed Norton's assistant in the sewer," he said.

"But those sewer workers are exposed to all those rats and all that filth," I sputtered.

"But, Audrey," he positively chirped, "I've worked in Hollywood for years. I've seen worse filth and worked with bigger rats."

★ SNAPSHOT ★

Ladies will recall that not so very long ago any man compared with Robert Taylor would qualify for Superhunk, virile, charming, with demanding eyes and a voice with muscles. He was not only a splendid actor in a wide variety of roles but one of the most handsome men in the Western world.

Bob Taylor was one of the few people who didn't accept that judgment and remained a friendly, no-airs nice guy known and liked by a lot of people, including Jackie Gleason.

And Jackie had a favor to ask of his friend Robert Taylor.

It seemed that one of Jackie's top sponsors had a niece who was entranced with Taylor. She was a shy, fragile young woman but if Bob could meet her at Jackie's place for just a few minutes of small talk, her world would wear wings, the sponsor would be beholden, and Jackie would be most grateful.

Anything for a pal. Taylor arrived to meet the timid but anxious young lady and did his best in stilted but enthusiastic banter as she positively piped inanities while smoothing the folds of her prim, floor-length evening gown.

Abruptly, she decided she must leave. Taylor and Gleason rose in gentlemanly fashion, and the lady turned and made her exit. The dress had a prim front, but the back was missing from the waist down, and Robert Taylor was thoroughly mooned by Jackie's paid performer.

Jackie said Bob Taylor wanted to kill him, but they were both laughing too hard for him to be a decent target, or for Taylor to throw a punch.

★ SNAPSHOT ★

One day at rehearsal Jack Philbin took me aside and said, "Don't look now, but there is a man sitting up in the balcony—don't look, I said. He has been coming on Saturdays to watch rehearsals, and he's been watching you and would like to take you out."

I sputtered, "Take me out? I don't go on blind dates with anyone! Much less anyone sitting up in the balcony in the dark!"

Philbin smiled and said, "Don't you want to know who he is?"

"I couldn't care less," said I, tossing my head in prim disdain, and started to walk away.

Philbin, loath to give up, said, "He's James Michener."

I spun around. "The author? Oh, I'd love to meet him. I'm a big fan."

We were properly introduced, and he asked me out. We went to El Morocco, and my evening was like a grilling at a precinct house by New York's Finest. I've never been asked so many nonstop questions in my life, about my family, childhood, et cetera. He was a lovely guy—courteous, charming, fascinating, but alarmingly curious. He wanted to know everything you knew, I guess for literary characters waiting to be born. I'm still waiting to meet myself in his next book. Hopefully, I will be courteous, charming, and fascinating too!

One of These Days, Alice

A lot of Hollywood people became fascinated with "The Honeymooners" and taken with the idea of doing a one-time guest appearance. Rosalind Russell was sure she was right for some unknown lady upstairs who could play beautifully in a sketch. Sleek, tart-tongued, graceful Roz, in a Bensonhurst walk-up! C'mon!

"And you were born and bred in Flatbush, right?" she responded to my disbelief.

She didn't push seriously for a part, but her reminder of how I'd had to swim upstream to play Alice told me that assuming dimensions of talent is a shaky bet. Jackie Gleason, as a serious actor and as a composer and conductor? Whaddaya think were the odds?

Well, one of Hollywood's leading lights and, Lord knows, comedy's, arrived when Jack Benny came to the studio to play the Kramdens' cheap landlord in one show

Before his arrival, Jackie called Joan Reichman to his dressing room.

"You know, Joan, how immaculate and fastidious Benny is—he's the neatest man I've ever met. So I want you to find a spot backstage to put up some flats and make a phony dressing room for him. Throw all the trash you can find in there, get Cuoco to make some spiderwebs, put up a cracked mirror, and do it fast. Then put a great big star on the door."

Joan was equal to the occasion, and when Benny appeared everyone was very respectful to one of the greatest comedians of our time. Almost ceremoniously, Jackie led him to his dressing room, which now was emblazoned with a huge star. Benny, embarrassed, and more than a little nonplussed by all this reverential treatment from fellow actors, opened the door to find Instant Slum: cracked mirror, broken chair, littered floor, old bottles, sandwich remnants, sagging cartons of anonymous stuff. . . .

"Mr. Benny," intoned Jackie, "welcome to your dressing room."

Benny very nearly collapsed with laughter. He had been properly set up for the payoff kick in the pants and loved it. His real dressing room was most suitable, and he was a great pro to work with in the scene. Off camera, though, he kept going back to that first dressing room for another look and a chuckle. I'm sure he liked it, because he didn't look pensive and give a four-beat drawling, "Well . . ."

Jack Benny was one of America's treasures. A Sunday-night landmark of network radio, his television shows were actually his radio sequences with pictures. He was one of the few whose characters were so vivid that he made the transition from sound to sight-and-sound without missing a step.

I was so pleased when he asked me to come to California to be on his show in January 1958. A sweet and gracious man, he had created a character as the nation's most famous skinflint when he was actually a generous boss and a heavy tipper. But I found that he did have his fiscal problems when I had dinner with Jack and wife Mary Livingstone, plus producer Bill Goetz and wife Edie.

Mary Benny did not go out much at this time, so I was delighted when Jack said she was joining us. I drove to the Benny house to pick them both up in my rented station wagon, and we went to LaRue's restaurant. Mary filled me in on all the current Hollywood gossip. She destroyed my illusions completely about Rock Hudson many years before it became public knowledge.

We had a great time at dinner. Came the bill, and host Jack began to review the tab, line by line, while still conversing with the group. "Watch this," whispered Mary to me. After many minutes of bookkeeping, he handed the bill to Mary and almost plaintively asked, "How much should I tip?" She said, "He does this all the time." Jack wanted so much to be bountiful to the waiter, but he couldn't figure out what was munificent and what was cheap.

On the way home, Mary said she didn't go to New York much, but Jack liked to go for all the big openings, and when he did would I go out with him? I said, "Of course," delighted.

Back to rehearsals. The night we taped the show, director Semour Berns had sent me an old-fashioned nosegay, complete with roses, lace, and a stem to hold it by. I was touched because in New York you do a show and nobody sees you leave. In California they send flowers to your dressing room.

When the show was over, I asked my manager, Val Ir

ving, to call Jack in so I could say good-bye. I was wearing a black dress and long black gloves. I stretched out flat on the chaise longue, clutching the nosegay, as Val ushered Benny into the room, saying, "Audrey wants to say farewell." Benny collapsed on the floor hysterical. He was always the greatest audience for a gag.

Now we dissolve. Jack came to New York for the opening of *My Fair Lady*. He took me to dinner at "21" beforehand, and when the check arrived he was studying it and talking to me at the same time. You guessed it.... He handed the bill to me and said, "How much shall I tip? Mary always does this for me."

Jack took me to many openings, and it was possibly after *The Sound of Music* that we went to the Waldorf-Astoria. Eddie Fisher was opening there during the time that he was married to Elizabeth Taylor, so it was a very glamorous opening. Also, a very late evening. On the way home in the limo, Jack said, "Would you mind if I stop at a deli? I want to pick up some corn flakes and milk." "No problem," I replied. When we arrived at my apartment he said, "I'll just see you to your door." As we stepped out of the elevator and I was getting my key from my purse, I turned to thank him for the evening. Just like a little boy holding a paper sack, he said, "Could you loan me a bowl and a spoon?" Could I? Wouldn't you? I gave him a kitchen bowl and spoon, and he went off happily into the night. I never asked if he was going to eat his cereal because of the late night or if he was going to beat the hotel out of a breakfast check because no one was with him to tell him how much to tip. I rather imagine it was the former.

Merv Griffin was one of our guest singers in the first season of "The Honeymooners," but he knew Jackie before any of

Known for his great reactions, Jackie even upstaged my kiss.

CBS

Marilyn Monroe and Joe DiMaggio celebrate Jackie's fortieth birthday.

The three of us with Jackie's beauties—I wish I still had that coat.

Waiting patiently for rehearsal.

Six shows a day at the
Paramount—but we
never got to see
the movie!

Dennis Day and Jack Benny,
as Norton and Ralph, dine
at Chauncey Street.
The hostess appears to be
counting the silver.

The opening night party of a Broadway show I attended was given at the Automat.
Jack Benny is handing me a quarter to buy my dinner.

Al Hirschfeld accurately captured Jackie's famous "macaroni take."

Couldn't miss the opportunity to sneak in a hug between takes on *That Touch of Mink* with the gorgeous Cary Grant.

This Honeymooners postcard from the eighties featured Alice in a familiar pose.

I Can't Wait Till They Invent:

Frozen Dinners

Diet Soda

Women's Lib

Art and I, working on a "Honeymooners" special, laugh over a little "tongue-in-cheek."

This is the last picture of Jackie and me together. We were in Miami announcing the coming release of the "lost episodes."

Love, Alice

the rest of us did. They'd met during the Korean War, when Merv was a young band singer with a not so spectacular band in New York and Jackie went to see him at the club. Going to report for induction into the army the next day, Merv was feeling low about his departure from his singing career when Jackie used these words to console him: "Cheer up, reveille's going to sound a lot better to you than that band you're singing with." (This has nothing to do with "The Honeymooners," but almost fifty years later, Merv told me the story as one he recalls, over the clutter of time, as an example of Gleason's tilted view of life's sweet promise.)

One of Jackie's favorite personal stories illustrates his zany side. Seems he was working in a carnival somewhere, sometime, in his random ascent of the rungs of Show Business, in which a specialty act of elephants performed a miniature baseball game wearing outsize baseball bats and mitts. (No, I don't know how elephants did this. Jackie didn't let me interrupt either.)

The pitcher elephant bowled the ball. The batter hit it. The fielder butted it toward first. The batter ran. Well, you just had to be there, that's all. If anyone paid half a buck to see this extravaganza, I can make a fortune by putting my cousin on the road since he can crack his knuckles to "The Skaters' Waltz."

Anyway, Jackie decided to see if "Elephants never forget" was fact or fiction. With a couple of other disturbers of the peace and public order, he switched all the outsize elephant equipment to different jumbos. You're still with me, right? So, the next day, the catcher elephant can't recall how to catch without his chest protector. First baseman can't see through the catcher's mask, batter can't hit without the bat, and the pitcher can't pitch with a bat.

Animal psychologist Gleason discovered that, aha, elephants do indeed forget. But, aha, carnival managers do not forget, and he was excused from further salary checks.

It occurred to me that Lou Gehrig couldn't play first base with a catcher's mask on, and if the catcher didn't have a mask, he would have a fractured jaw before the seventh inning stretch. Exasperated, Jackie told me I knew nothing about baseball, or animals. I should have tipped our writers to this cosmic discussion. Fade-out.

One of Jackie's greatest takes was the simulation of pain. How many times did he supposedly slam the sliding window onto his fingers, then do three minutes of facial torment while crashing about the kitchen holding the paw of a wounded lion, bleating agony while the crowd roared? One night the pain was real. As I recall it, Jackie didn't like some of the sketches. He decided to write the main one over himself. The writers didn't like the act and had told him so, which made him even more determined to make it a topper. It required him to skate on dry ice in a Buster Brown outfit. Halfway through the sketch, he fell and Buster Browned his leg. They had to take him offstage on a stretcher. As they rolled him to the ambulance, he looked up at Leonard and said, "Don't say a word."

With Jackie out for repairs, he bought two sketches for Art and me as fill-ins until he could return. This was a usual practice when the star was ill. I read the first one and knew it was absolutely wrong for me. I was to be an overbearing woman boss puffing on a big cigar, who was cruel and ruthless to her frightened, wimpish secretary, who was, of course, Art Carney. I told Val I didn't want to do it. The second sketch wasn't great, but it was not totally wrong for me, so I agreed to play it.

Bullets and all the king's horses of MCA told Val that if I did not do both sketches, I would be let go. I felt so strongly about it I told Val to relay to Bullets that it was okay with me. I said, "I'll give them two weeks' notice, but if they can't find someone to replace me in two weeks, naturally I won't leave them hanging."

This must have been relayed to Jackie, because he was the next one on the phone.

"Aud, Aud, you gotta do it, you'll be a riot!"

I said, "I'll not only not be a riot, I'll probably never work again. The audience will come up onstage and get me."

He said, "Just do it for me this time, and if I'm wrong and it's not great, next time I'll listen to you."

Wearily, I said, "Jackie, if I do that sketch, there won't be a next time. You know, to make it funny, that's a part for Martha Raye or Nancy Walker, not me. But I will do the other sketch under duress."

He gave up then and said, "Okay, but I think you're a clam."

There was no more talk about letting me go. That Saturday I did the other sketch, which was a satire on "Dorothy and Dick's" breakfast radio show with Art. It didn't exactly lay there, but it was not hilarious either.

The broken leg was tolerated as an inconvenience rather than a barrier, and Jackie was back calling the shots in a plaster cast, with a cane, despite the contrary minds of medical science. He found it awkward yet not impossible to keep the nightlife of New York up to major league standards and to ensure that the liquor industry did not recede into hard times.

As we know from our Shakespeare, wherever wine is, wenches cannot be far distant. Jackie used to tell me about some of his misadventures in the way you might chat to your favorite girl cousin, or your friend's wife—not putting a verbal move on, just sharing bits of wackiness that was more funny than carnal.

One night, having imbibed more than usual, Jackie with two of his buddies decided it would be nice to have some girls along. In the numbing crush of a late, late evening, they found some willing companions at the bar. Jackie said, "I'll take the blonde, you guys can have the brunette and redhead," and staggered to the door.

When he arrived at his apartment with the blonde in question—or is it Questionable Blonde?—she insisted they had to play butcher shop. Jackie was fast approaching the point when he couldn't have played touch your nose with two fingers, so he was unready for games. But, if he didn't play the game, he couldn't win the prize, which, presumably, was her living, breathing self.

What the heck? "How d'ya play?" "Well, I'm the customer, you're the butcher. I order meat from you, lamb chops, steaks, et cetera. I say, 'How much is that?' and you say, 'That will be thirty-five dollars.' I say, 'Oh, dear, I don't have any money.' Then you'll have to jump on my bones for the money." Curtain.

Is this snappy theatre or what? He didn't tell me how many lamb chops he bought. Come to think of it, he'd swallowed a lake of Scotch that night, and he didn't tell me if he found himself a vegetarian.

One of the next vice squad pinups Jackie brought home removed enough clothing to prove that the Park Sheraton had central heating. Then she said, "We're going to play auction. You'll have to bid on me."

Jackie looked around to find the rest of the bidding crowd, but the object of the bidding had turned into her own auctioneer and was calling the action.

Presumably, the easy chair bid fifty bucks, the dresser

went for seventy-five, Jackie went for one hundred (beats the lamb chops, right?), and the mirror and the book rack were really into it, going higher and higher, according to the auctioneer, who was so excited she threw in a bid herself, just to keep the action popping.

Unlike the passionate auctioneer, the only other live person on the premises had become uncommonly drowsy since once again he had come close to drinking vast portions of Manhattan dry. "Also," he said, "I was getting dizzy walking around her, bidding in different voices, so I severely cut the allowances of the mirror and the book rack, and she was in for a big surprise."

He wandered off, to deep and solitary sleep, in his bedroom while the woman apparently marched off to other auctions with that lethal notice "No Acceptable Bid."

Phil Cuoco, Sancho Panza to Don Quixote Gleason, recalled a brush with hedonism in staid Boston, when they were there for some function. Late in the evening, both hungry (and without doubt, thirsty), they discovered a nightery unmentioned in *Recommended Tours of the Athens of America*. It appeared to be operated by a management whose individual noses had suffered great violence and whose significant bulges in the neighborhood of shoulder holsters told you that this was not Maxim's alumni.

Recognizing Jackie, the ownership were pleased indeed and insisted on comping the drinks and meals, while the twelve-girl chorus of twelve—count them, twelve—fought one another for space on the postage stamp stage. (Phil insisted they were not dancers. He called them walkers.) Naturally, Jackie and Phil applauded and cheered. Hey, they were fellow performers, weren't they? As the boys got up to leave, one of the muscles in suits hissed to Jackie, "Which girl do you want me to send over to you tonight?"

And Jackie, being Jackie, roared, "All of them!"

Back at the very proper Copley Plaza Hotel, he summoned the two night managers in their cutaways and striped pants. "Please add $1,200 to my bill as a cash expense," he instructed formally. "About 3:00 A.M., twelve lovely girls are going to come in and ask for me. Give each of them $100. Tell them they had a great time and send them home."

As previously noted, Jackie was casual about cash, which made Phil's job as scenic designer, property manager, and official companion to the Star a source of large stories but small rewards. Having invited two visitors to shoot a game of Chicago, or rotation, or whatever variation of pocket billiards he thought seasonal for the evening, Jackie found he was temporarily wagerless after challenging the duo for $100 each.

They appeared unlikely hustlers, dressed in long, baggy shorts, kneesocks, and oxfords. Jackie used his corner-of-the-mouth growl to assure Phil that "these hunkies" were "cold cuts" and that Phil should pop for two hundred in order to commence the slaughter of the innocents with the semihandcuffed Phil as his partner. Jackie called his shots and sank them as Phil beamed and the hunkies looked for doors.

After "The Honeymooners" team was victorious and the losers paid up, Phil suggested it would be nice if Jackie repaid him the entry fee plus his share of the winnings.

"You don't mean you want to rob the poor box," screamed a shocked Gleason. "Those guys are priests from New Jersey!"

Phil never did get his loan back, nor is there a firm record that the parish poor box in New Jersey lit up the Cheerful Giver Board. When Jackie was on a roll, he couldn't spare time for bookkeeping.

Love, Alice

In 1950s New York, to *mitt* meant to tip, usually people one wasn't required to tip. Our Jackie had the practice of mitting everyone capable of breathing in and out when he was in a place of food, drink, and merriment. Children of busboys, saxophonists, cleaning ladies, people who opened doors, people who closed doors, people who helped push revolving doors, all made it through part of a semester of college if Jackie visited their parents' place of business with any kind of regularity.

In a Miami seafood restaurant, he had mitted everyone but the guy who catches the oysters. Comfortably tapped out, he was enjoying a show-tune medley by the bar piano player. Faithful Phil, of course, was at his side.

"Put ten bucks in the fishbowl on the piano as a vote of confidence to the musician," Jackie suggested.

Phil complied. Half an hour later, Jackie proposed that Phil donate another sawbuck to the bowl of the new Bobby Short. Aware that this could become a long and costly night, Phil said, "I just mitted the guy with a ten half an hour ago."

Jackie gathered his face into the aghast position. "That was my ten-dollar tip," he enunciated carefully for any slow learners. "This ten dollars is yours."

Phil was not only faithful but also a friend who, repeatedly, risked his life in Jackie's company—he consented to be a passenger in an automobile in motion when Jackie was at the wheel.

Jackie was not a bad driver. He was the worst driver, of any city, state, or nation. Physically, he was as coordinated as an athlete. Behind the wheel, he waged and lost a war with every internal-combustion-powered item of machinery ever assembled. If he could turn on the radio and work the cigarette lighter, it had been a good day. Turning left required speed and courage in large amounts. Shifting gears was done best with the manual open on his lap. Parallel parking was for nuclear physicists.

Jackie had grown up so poor that he was lucky his mother worked for the subway or he would have had trouble coming up with two nickels for a round trip from Bushwick. With no car in the family, he never really learned how to drive. He used to tell us about early emcee dates in New Jersey when he'd be driven by a friend who was mostly blind, while Jackie could see but couldn't drive. If he could have just retold the story of him playing Seeing Eye dog for the unseeing man at the wheel, he would have had the audience in hysterics. Anyway, Jackie, obviously, never got behind the wheel in his teens or even early twenties. In fact, judging from events in later life, he may have decided to move from pedestrian to Indianapolis 500 finalist without any baby steps. Here are a few recollections of Ralph Kramden at the wheel.

Good man Phil Cuoco insists that whatever Jackie thought about his driving abilities, Phil and agent Jerry Katz were formally assigned to teach him to drive (this would be in 1955 or so). Phil's succinct report on teaching Jackie to drive: "The fact that we survived was a miracle."

Now Jackie had to pass the road test for his state license. They didn't dare risk him in Manhattan traffic. Off they went to Long Island—specifically Mineola, county seat of Nassau County, adjoining Queens. At the test site, Jerry slipped out from behind the wheel and Jackie took his place. The Motor Vehicle Bureau inspector was amazed and delighted to find that the Great Mr. Gleason would be reviewed by himself.

> **INSPECTOR:** Oh, Mr. Gleason, we watch all your shows. My wife would just love to get your autograph.

JACKIE: Okay, pal. Soon as we finish, I'll give you a great big one for the Little Woman.
INSPECTOR: Oh, thank you. That'll be very nice. You may proceed.
JACKIE: And awaaay we go!

Right into reverse and into the radiator of the car behind him. The front of the car is weeping water through its smashed grill as the hood snaps open to block sight of the frenzied driver. Phil and Jerry are turned to stone on the sidewalk. Everyone else in the area is making crowd noises and doing war dances. Jackie yells to the smashed car that he'll take care of everything, and he and the inspector proceed.

The inspector gets an autograph you could frame for a gallery inscribed to Mrs. Inspector, plus Jackie's own Harvard red carnation for pressing in her memory book. The guy with the sick car gets well quickly when he finds that he was lucky enough to have a person of means bash his tin.

And, God save us all, Jackie gets his driver's license.

Later, Jackie had a gorgeous customized Cadillac with the control panel of a 747 and a backseat fit for light housekeeping for a family of four. It was a lot of car, a lot too much for its driver.

Somehow, he got to Columbus Circle from the Park Sheraton (a couple of blocks) and turned and turned . . . and turned . . . and, well, you get the picture. What do you do at a circle, right? Turn.

This Cadillac had a mind of its own, and it seemed to have this thing for Columbus Circle. The other cars presumed that the steering wheel was stuck, or the driver was dotty, or dead, and started to take violent and erratic action to get away from this persistent red monster swinging around at them like a perpetual motion machine. People seeking to cross the street ran into Central Park or down the subway steps, or clung to light poles, waiting for a final horrendous smashup.

Somewhere in the Golden Book, it is written how many times Jackie Gleason whirled his Cadillac around Columbus Circle, but at least he managed to run it into and over a curb and return the circle to New York City, and to Columbus. Being Jackie, he then phoned his office and bellowed, "Call Cadillac and tell them to get this wreck out of here." The man had a way with words. Not machines.

A PR fellow we all liked had gotten a new client and was most anxious for Jackie to display his product on the show—a cute little Nash Metropolitan. Since that Nash was built for an average person, and at that time Jackie was two average persons, it took extraordinary effort to jam him into the driver's seat, and then, oh boy, did he awaaay we go! Audible prayers were offered to a variety of gods in desperate tones as Our Leader whirled onto the stage and roared toward tense cameramen, anxious floor managers, and an unsuspecting audience wildly applauding as the Jackiemobile aimed for them, the driver cheerfully waving.

In one of the great proofs of the existence of the supernatural, the Nash stopped eighteen inches from running out of stage, and Jackie managed to pop out like a champagne cork. The audience's cheers drowned out the fervent thank-yous of cast and crew to reliable saints and spirits.

And it came to pass that because Mr. Gleason had been so accommodating, Mr. Nash (or his inheritors) saw to it that he received two of the little cars for his very own. New Yorkers fled indoors!

Since you are already pretty clear on the point that Jackie was a danger to the population of North America while behind the wheel, I'll reassure you by noting that he did not drive fast nor did he ever hit people or things (that we know of) in his life on the open road. But writer Leonard Stern recalls, with discomfort to this day, the time Jackie insisted on giving Leonard a lift to Jackie's place in Peekskill.

The mode of transportation was the itsy-bitsy Nash Metropolitan (possibly made under subcontract from Tinkertoys), which would include Leonard, a larger-than-large Jackie, and Jackie's man, Tony, who also occupied generous areas of which this automobile was deficient. Mr. Gleason, of course, was navigator and pilot. Passengers Tony and Leonard attempted to arrange body parts to fit the remaining space of the Nash container.

The master motorist reached a decision. There was too much humanity for the vehicle. Answer: Drive with the motorist's door half open. And that's how they tooled along the highways, Jackie chatting with one- and two-handed gestures while one foot held the driver's door open and the other toyed with accelerator and brake. It was a routine trip of several thousand miles, I presume, because Leonard never requested a ride with Jackie again.

My own most memorable experience as a passenger with Our Jackie at the wheel occurred when we decided to visit some friends playing in a Manhattan theatre a few blocks away. Since I was dimly aware of his reputation as a driver who laughed at danger because he was confounded by the difference between the manual shift and the windshield washer, I presumed we would walk the few blocks or take a cab. But, no, the garage had delivered his shiny new Buick to the curb just for us, and any excuse I sought seemed inadequate, cowardly, contemptible. That wouldn't have stopped me, of course, if I'd thought I would save myself from a trip for two over a cliff, but what could happen in a few blocks, huh? Read on.

There were no collisions, no traffic infractions, no oral violence with other drivers infringing on Gleason's side of the street, and we arrived at the theatre. But there were also no parking places. Once around the block. Twice around the block. Everyone had parked his car here and gone to Long Island for the summer, Jackie considered. Halfway around the block once more, and Jackie spotted the huge double doors of the rear of the theatre, where scenery and freight were unloaded.

"We've found our parking place, Aud!" he trilled, and whirled us over the curb, up the loading ramp, and, with a harsh complaint of brakes looking for asphalt and finding the ancient boards of stage center, we made our entrance as people in and out of costume leaped for the orchestra pit or the curtain at top speed.

Of course, Jackie talked his way out of everything while I concentrated on smiling graciously, and willing my heart to stop beating in time to the *William Tell Overture*. As Jackie noted later, "It was only a run-through, not a performance, and they didn't have to give any refunds."

From Jackie, that translated to "All's well that ends well."

Let us all agree that not even Jackie had faith in himself as a chauffeur. But when it came to stage presence and stage timing, he was top of the bill, all the time, every time. He expected to be, and, after a very little bit, we were as sure of him as he was.

For instance. Most everybody on the show recalls the pie in the face routine with three actors in motion, accomplished with no rehearsal. For openers, I'll agree that pie in the face is not Strindberg, or Chekhov, and not even George S. Kaufman. Its genesis is more baggy pants and squirting seltzer bottles than, say, the shaded drolleries of a Shavian plot. But you put three actors into this bit of boffo business and you are attempting a pro football triple reverse. And those guys practice every day and still lose ten yards, if they don't fumble on that play.

The story line had Ralph and Norton entering an amateur contest, and their act was to be Laurel and Hardy, with Jackie as a waiter and Art the customer. They looked incredibly like the originals! Rehearsing lines but not action in the kitchen set, the dialogue went something like this:

> **JACKIE:** What can I do for you?
> **ART:** I'd like a piece of custard pie.
> **JACKIE:** The customer is always right. I'm sorry to say we're all out of custard pie. But we do have a whipped cream blueberry pie.
> **ART:** But I don't happen to care for whipped cream blueberry pie. I'm the customer, and I want a custard pie.
> **JACKIE:** But this is a very good whipped cream blueberry pie.
> **ART:** I don't care how good it is, I want custard pie. Now let me have it. Wait a minute, Ralph.
> **JACKIE:** Norton, you don't have room to say, "Let me have it" and "Wait a minute"!
> **ART:** We don't have to do it now, we can do it tomorrow at the show.
> **JACKIE:** Say: Let me have it, Norton!
> **ART** (weeping): I don't want to!
> **JACKIE:** Say: Let me have it!
> **ART:** All right. Let me have it.
> **JACKIE:** All right!

Alice had exited to the bedroom, so Jackie said, "Aud, can you see me from there when I cock my arm?"

I said, "Yes." So he told me when I saw that, to walk on-stage. Art would duck, and the pie would get me in the face as I walked out. What confidence! On the air I did exactly that—it was timed perfectly. The pie hit me dead center, and, of course, the audience roared. (Why not? They hadn't been hit.) Unfortunately, however, Props had felt sorry for me getting the pie, so they had flavored the whipped cream with vanilla so it would taste good. That it did, but the vanilla stung and reddened my eyes, the whipped cream soaked my hair, and I had two more scenes to do.

In live TV, you cannot stop to dry your hair. Happily, in the next scene, I wore a long black wig and Hawaiian costume singing "Little Grass Shack," with Joyce dressed as a sailor accompanying me on the banjo, since we had also entered the contest. But the last scene was back in the kitchen. I was frantic about what to do about my hair till I saw a strange woman standing in the wings. Jackie's luck was with me. She was wearing a scarf.

I snatched it, saying, "Can I borrow this for a minute? Thank you," and on the stage I went. So if you ever plan to catch a pie in the face, lose the vanilla. You'll thank me for it.

To reinforce what so many people find hard to believe about our haphazard rehearsals, I must tell you about an earlier scene in this same show. You know the plotline about the contest.

In the first scene, Ralph and Alice have an argument in which Ralph tells Alice she can't go in the contest doing her hula number. Alice insists she's not only going to enter but she's going to win because she has a big finish.

RALPH: Oh yeah, can I see it?
ALICE: I'll be very happy to show you.

With which, I stood on my head on one of the kitchen chairs and sang "Il Bacio" upside down. I had to do the headstand on a chair for the camera angle to get the shot. I asked Art to be sure to stand behind the chair to catch my legs so I wouldn't flip completely over. At rehearsal, I flung myself upside down on the chair, and there was no music. Ray Bloch, our conductor, was standing there with his arms folded.

Jackie roared, "Where's the music?"

"You mean she can sing that upside down?" asked Ray, dumbfounded.

He thought it would be dubbed with someone offstage. Jackie, in his casual way, had forgotten to tell him. Anyway, on the air the intro was there, Art caught my legs to brace me upside down, I sang the number, and the applause was thunderous for the upside-down performer.

Another famous Saturday, Jackie threw out a scene in the middle of the afternoon. What to replace it with? Get on the phone and call his pals to play in a pickup band with me as the band singer, singing "Make Love to Me." As Steve Allen describes it, "The pickup band was more like a rotten band that no one would pick up." The phone calls produced Jack Carter on bass; Phil Silvers on clarinet; Steve Allen, obviously, on piano; Garry Moore on drums; Jack Lescoulie, our announcer, on trombone; and Jackie on trumpet. And another glorious moment from TV's Golden Age was born.

As Steve said later, "Some of Jackie's routine things got very loose around the edges, but with his warmth, charisma, and anything-goes style, he could make it work."

Either the band stopped too soon or we never decided on one chorus or two. They stopped, and I went on singing. The band revived, came back in, and we all triumphantly finished together.

Again to quote Steve, "On live TV you saw the terrible and the great, sometimes all in one evening."

The writers stayed hot, and, therefore, so did "The Honeymooners." Actors are not shrinking violets or we would never have the nerve to get up on a stage and play an adult version of let's pretend before an audience not made up of our families. Each of us had talent and seasoning and a personal style, but we also needed the men with the words to stitch character and plot together every Saturday. Jackie, as I said earlier, was one of the few comics who appreciated that fact. He once emphasized the need for great writing by telling me, "Juliet is a great part, but if she'd played the balcony scene by saying, 'Why doesn't Romeo call me anymore?' instead of all that 'wherefore' stuff, she'd have been selling orange soda in the lobby during the intermission."

He had that right, even though he liked to put me on a bit about his lack of theatre knowledge. When the mood took him, he could roll off Shakespearean soliloquies seldom heard in Bushwick but absorbed in his vast reading.

When you shoot any show live, every action will not come out as ordained by writer and director. There often proved to be an invisible presence on set who rearranged the poor actor's life.

In one show, Ralph's line was "We're all going to drink a toast" as he twisted the cork from a bottle of champagne. The cork refused its cue, and we stood there with glasses high and smiles wan while Jackie wrestled the wine, finally choking out "if I can ever get this thing open," which earned him a laugh. The audience appreciated being part of an inside gag, especially a malfunctioning prop. In another episode, Alice had arranged a fancy table setting, complete with wineglasses. Ralph lifted the fragile glass, sneering, "What's this for, sauerkraut juice?" and set it down harder than he'd planned, shattering it. Jackie was dumbfounded that a prop glass had broken, and I had to cover with "Just for that, you're not getting anything to drink."

Door problems seem to have plagued people ever since we all moved out of caves and got doors for our trouble. They certainly have troubled actors. The set can be exquisite, costumes brilliant, troupe perfectly cast. But when the stage center door gets stuck, so too do the Company of Players. Windy and nonsensical phrases leap to palsied lips of marooned actors desperately inventing dialogue, or pieces of business, as the behind-the-scenes crew use anxious hands, edged tools, and awful curses on the door born in hell.

Of course, it happened to me as the only one left onstage, but, as I recall with clarity, while Jackie made his exit, hearing an ominous click as the door slammed. I thought there couldn't possibly be a lock on that door, no reason for it, but there was. Art was to enter next, but all I could hear were people jiggling the knob back and forth and whispering. Meanwhile, left all alone onstage, I resisted the temptation to exit myself through the bedroom door. I hummed my way over to the stove and started to put a pot on, stirring nothing furiously. Consequently, my back was to the window. It seemed as though an hour had gone by—it was probably a few seconds—when I turned to see Art coming through the window saying, "There's more than one way to skin a cat." He had forgotten to open the window, since there was naturally no glass in it. Jackie had sent him around to the Kramden fire escape outside our window, hissing, "Run, Aud can't stall out there forever." The next one supposed to enter was a Western Union boy. He knocked, and as I started for the door, Art said, "Good luck." The studio audience had caught on by now that the door had turned into concrete, and they loved it. Yet this time it opened to applause for the door, and, thank God, another live TV crisis was over.

As noted, Jackie's Civil War style meant to follow him and improvise as we lunged into a wonder world while on camera, ignited by his sudden intuitive rush of how the scene would play bigger, better, brighter. He had magnificent instincts and superior luck. Time after time, Jackie reached into his grab bag, and we all shared gold.

Yet, as must happen to all men, one time Jackie thought he'd been hit by lightning, when, alas, it was only a cramp. He wanted to develop new characters for himself and Art. Jackie wrote a sketch for them called "The Clam Diggers." They were supposed to be vendors on Coney Island who paused to meet with their shellfish carts to chew the fat, but it was not very well constructed. Art's ESP must have been working, because he had visited one of his brothers, who was a dentist, and had him fashion a set of false buck teeth for his character. They didn't help.

I watched from the wings as the scene became a dive off the ten-meter board into an empty pool and the audience faded from smiles to coughs. The only things missing were a premise, a beginning, a middle, and an end. Flop sweat became a danger to sound footing.

I was so sorry for my pals, but so happy that I was not dying a horrible death among them that I bolted before they started reciting the Lord's Prayer for a big finish. I laughed all the way home in the cab, only slightly manic that I had been saved by a Greater Power from having been a part of that Custer Massacre. When I asked Jackie the next day how he planned to rewrite "The Clam Diggers," he said, "I have very bad news. Both of them drowned in the Coney Island surf. No one cried, including me."

We filmed the thirty-nine shows at DuMont because Dr. DuMont had perfected a new system called the Electronicam, which was the precursor of videotape. Consequently, we had to use his system, although we were still with CBS. Jackie had one rule which was inviolable: "When the camera is going, the action is going. We won't stop for anything; we'll do it exactly the same as the live show. If anything goes radically wrong, we'll finish that script for the audience and then put the script away for five or six weeks so we can come back to it fresh. We will not ever do anything over!"

As I mentioned, any live show combining the talents of twenty or thirty actors and technicians, which is first cousin to a Broadway opening every week, is not going to run like a Swiss watch. Besides, we found that the people in the theatre audience were not only forgiving but actually pleased to be insiders if they caught a gaffe now and then.

One night, though, we topped ourselves. Fluffing a line or dropping a prop was nothing compared with our theatrical shambles. "Better Living Through TV" was the script in which Jackie and Art go on TV to sell a can opener that could also "core a apple." (The premise of many shows was Ralph coming up with a new get-rich-quick scheme and dragging Norton along.) Now, a stage wall is known as a flat and is forever being repainted and moved about to be a wall of a living room, or a garden, or a castle, or a barbershop, or even a kitchen. At the end of the scene, as Jackie was doing his pain bit, he accidentally hit the flat, which was not anchored solidly, and it went over on the floor, with Jackie flat on his face. Art went to help him, and he fell too.

True to form, there was no retake, and to this day when you see a rerun of "Better Living Through TV," you'll see them finish on the floor. The studio audience loved it. Me, too.

If you can make people laugh when the house is literally falling down, you've picked the right career. Today they would stop film or stop tape and do it over, eliminating all spontaneity. But in Jackie's Civil War leadership, the command was always "Charge!" We never reshot one single line in thirty-nine shows, and we did two half hours a week. A unique record, which I'm sure will never be matched.

Jackie was such a good actor that he somehow appeared to change sizes to fit his comedy characters. One of my favorite episodes was a Christmas show we did where I got to meet all Jackie's other characters in "The Honeymooners" kitchen—characters I had not worked with before. The premise was Ralph coming up from the neighborhood bar to tell Alice all the people who were there, The Loudmouth, The Poor Soul, Reggie Van Gleason, Charlie Bratton, and so on. All, he said, were at the bar.

They had all put The Poor Soul on by giving him a little rhinestone and telling him it was a diamond. Ralph would go back down, and one by one each character would come up to the kitchen to wish Alice a merry Christmas. When Jackie appeared as Reggie with a group of showgirls, he looked nine feet tall—with that towering top hat. But when he came in as The Poor Soul, he shrank before my eyes. It was a very touching scene. Alice sits him down and gives him cookies, Coke, sandwiches, a present, all of which he tries to balance on his knees, and when he has been fed, he pantomimes that he has something to give Alice. He starts unbuttoning his jacket, then his vest, then his shirt, till he gets down to a little change purse. He opens it and presents Alice with the rhinestone he thinks is a diamond. I was fascinated with how small Jackie could make himself seem by disappearing so completely into the character.

Another Christmas show, Jackie decided he would just be the emcee, and we would all have to do something different. I had to do a soft-shoe routine with June Taylor. June was such a great dancer, and she was choreographing a great number for us, which she could do with ease. But it was a different story for me. Finally, at rehearsal I said, "June, I better show you the steps I know, because I'll never learn yours by Saturday." So I stole a few from "I Still Get Jealous," the soft-shoe number in *High Button Shoes*, which she incorporated with hers so I wouldn't look a complete klutz, and we danced up a storm.

"The Honeymooners" built an unofficial repertory company during its time in the number-one spot. Indeed, it was in great part the skills and subtleties of these character actors who adapted to the Civil War leadership of Jackie and the freewheeling movement of the scripts which gave us the pace and energy that keeps the show fresh to this day. Jackie really appreciated what these performers brought to the show, so much so that he asked them to come in a variety of disguises.

George Petrie, a great favorite of all of us, wore wigs and mustaches, developed scars, found a German accent, played one scene without uttering a word (since he was supposed to have been stabbed to death). His wife, Pat, was also one of our mainstays, and when the Petries adopted a child, the writers came up with an adoption script with Pat as the nurse and George as the doctor.

This became one of our most famous shows. Ralph and Alice adopt a baby, and in the last scene the mother wants it back and we have to give it up. The public was so emotionally involved with the story that the CBS switchboard was tied up for about twenty-four hours with people calling to say we could keep the baby! Years later, we redid the show, for a special, as a musical in Miami. It remains one of my very favorites because it was so touching.

As Ralph Kramden's assistant bus dispatcher, George had a recognizable continuing role, but he could be a cop or a crook, a priest or a grocery clerk; with a change of hairstyle or costume, he was a new man. Or an old one.

He reminded me that my first year on the show, I'd ask him to stand in the wings to "hold the book, in case I go up." George said, "Audrey, I've wasted more theatre time in the wings waiting for you to fluff a line or miss a cue than I've spent trying to get jobs in the theatre." A resourceful and cheery guy and an excellent actor, but I needed the insurance.

Indeed, George was one of the select group who played poker with Jackie of an evening. Always a great host, Jackie wanted the players to eat as much as he was consuming during the game, but all held back lest they eat themselves away from the table. That never bothered the Host. George had worked with Edward Everett Horton onstage and had considered him the master comic actor, until he worked with Jackie. He didn't realize, until I told him, that Jackie considered Horton the greatest scene stealer in motion pictures. Obviously, Jackie had learned some of those close-up reaction takes from someone he too considered the best in the business.

A few years ago, a journalist interviewing me about Jackie asked a question he considered more profound than I did. It was "Don't you think there was a thin man crying to get out of the fat man?"

Love, Alice

My answer, "No, I don't think he heard any cries or lost a wink of sleep over the fact that he was heavy."

Now this may sound bananas after my reference to Jackie's sporadic dieting and the fact that he was, of course, aware of his size. But it wasn't any overriding problem in his life. He was good looking, witty, popular, rich, at the top of his professional life, a national celebrity who was beloved in his native New York. The fact that his married life was in terminal confusion wasn't due to his weight. Hard to believe, but he had been very slender as a teenager and well into his twenties. As a comic actor, he naturally used his weight to gain or build a laugh, and he was never reticent about using his size as a comic device in a script. All of us might yearn for the form divine, but with Jackie the yen never went very far beyond a three-day diet as a try at physical reconstruction.

I've also often heard both Art Carney and Jackie compared to Laurel and Hardy, and I couldn't disagree more. Stan Laurel was the initiator of trouble that befell Oliver Hardy. But Ralph Kramden (Hardy) was the zany idea man who inveigled Norton (Laurel); then the writers would redevelop the plotline together, with Alice and/or Trixie becoming integral players. Laurel and Hardy were one remove from Keystone Kops and in line with Our Gang in their physical kick-in-the-pants and tumble-down-the-stairs sight gags. Plots were almost extraneous to the physical action. It was, and is, funny, but it could almost be played without dialogue, as I'm sure it was when shown in some foreign countries. Slipping on a banana peel is international.

"The Honeymooners" was funny, too. But you wouldn't run ten barking dogs through the apartment set to illustrate a weirdo home sweet home, or have an Eskimo family liv ing in the icebox. Comedic situations of "The Honeymooners" shaped by ensemble acting and honed dialogue to overcome obstacles and resolve the plot are a country mile away from Stan's weeping and Ollie's shattered aplomb as they both are frantic quarry running from the Bad Guys in a hysterical chase scene through a railroad roundhouse. How come no one said Jackie and Art were like Abbott and Costello? Because Ollie was a big, fat man and so was Jackie. That's why.

The younger the journalist who interviews me, the more often I get the question, politely or provocatively, depending on the mien of the reporter, "Why didn't Alice get a job and be her own person instead of just being a wife to Ralph?" Alice did have three jobs in five years, as a babysitter, a secretary, and her old job in the bakery, but Ralph made her give them all up. But you had to start with normal contemporary situations or the audience wouldn't have known if these people—the Kramdens—were different from normal Brooklynites.

In the midfifties, a man with an average job owned a home and a car, supported wife and family, saved for his kids' education, and had many times more leisure hours available than he does today for family activities, sports, civic and fraternal clubs, sleep, sex, and just standing around. Women customarily worked until a year or two after they were married (their salary going into a nest egg for a house down payment or furniture), or until they became pregnant. Exceptions were schoolteachers, nurses, legions of clerical, retail, and telephone personnel, assembly workers, and, of course, entertainers, who would give up a blood transfusion before they would turn away from a last curtain call.

So, on *The Adventures of Ozzie & Harriet*, Harriet didn't

run General Motors in the afternoon, she watched over the Nelson boys' homework. And Jane Wyatt never got far from the kitchen because, as we know, "Father Knows Best." Lucy Ricardo always wanted to be a Big Something in Show Business, but Desi always wanted her *en la casa*, and that was part of the story structure.

So, too, with "The Honeymooners." Ralph would have been considered distinctly unusual if his wife worked when the spouses of all the other city bus drivers were housewives. There were discussions of various story lines over the years—Alice has a baby, Alice inherits a business, Alice wins a fancy model home. Never happened. When you are Numero Uno in television, only a fool or a philosopher starts to take the watch apart to see if he can make it tick differently. Besides, we had the best writers in the business.

If you have gotten this far in this most informal history, you will know that I have been earning my bread since I was a teenager in every variation of the theatre but mud wrestling. And I hope to work, as H. L. Mencken said, "until they have to carry me out on a door." I think it's wonderful that our smartest and most energetic women are now reaching the goals that their talents so richly merit. Yet there are a lot of women who find no reward in repetitive and soul-wrenching jobs, who must drag themselves into a despairing ache of toil each day just to help keep their families solvent.

I am no alumna of a prestigious academy, nor do I truly understand the maze of economic Parcheesi called international finance, which has required 50 percent of American parents to both work to keep the family afloat. And the fact that one half of the mothers of children under six years old have got to leave the kids somewhere, anywhere, to punch a time clock doesn't seem to me like a recipe for that happier and healthier America the politicians keep talking about.

We didn't think we were innocent or naive back in the fifties (we'd just won the biggest war there ever was, remember?), but it isn't just nostalgia that makes life then seem more controlled by those who were living it. There were more hours for you and fewer for "them." If you're keeping score on your personal happiness quotient, you'll want the big, big chunk of hours in the "you" column.

Okay, okay, I'm giving up the floor to all the deep thinkers, and social scientists, and experts, and advisers, because if we did "The Honeymooners" today, Ralph would be driving a bus days and Alice would be the night dispatcher; Norton would still be down in the sewer, and Trixie would be working in one, aboveground, waiting tables at the Café Clutch just to cover the monthly plastic. What happened?

Why was one salary enough in the fifties and two don't quite make it in the nineties? Who changed the rules and why? Did we ever have a vote to make life harder?

Of course, I don't respond to a journalist's question with my own musings. The reporter is there to get a story on you, or your show, and you speak fast and truly. Funny, if you like, but be sure you're square with the interviewer. This is a job, and any deviation from the facts will embarrass him or her and type you as a lip or a liar.

Jackie being Jackie was an absolute jewel with the press; since he was the boss, he never had to worry about being second-guessed. He was such a feast of stories and wisecracks and snappy quotes, he was great copy and always on the record. I didn't know a reporter who didn't enjoy him, and I mean enjoy, not just like him. He was Mr. Conviviality.

They even forgave him some wildies, such as the time

he put it out that Our Phil Cuoco was going to marry the statuesque songstress Peggy Lee at the Little Church Around the Corner. Naturally, he hadn't advised Phil and Peggy of the event, so they were the only ones missing when much of Manhattan's press corps descended on the center aisle the next day.

I guess I have been interviewed by hundreds of reporters over the years, and I am always amazed at how accurate their reports are when prepared under the stress of deadlines. In decades of working with the press, I've only been surprised and shocked once by something attributed to me which I never said. A freelance writer, who is a reputable and seasoned reporter, interviewed me for a national magazine long after we'd stopped filming "The Honeymooners," and I told him some stories about Jackie and the old days. The writer discovered when he got his advance copy that, to give the article a little more bite, an editor three thousand miles away had made up quotes for me which demeaned Jackie. He was mortified when he told me about this mischief. In fact, he felt so badly that my irritation melted as I tried to calm him. What can a freelance writer do to an editor who commits the foul? Nothing, if he ever wants to get another assignment. I let it go because the writer was on the spot, but those fabricated quotes still annoy me.

They wouldn't Jackie. He'd give a lopsided grin and bark a harsh har-de-har-har and say something like "Let's talk seriously or let's drink seriously. Leave the bad guys for the sweepers. They'll find them soon enough. Your very good health, Mrs. Kramden."

"And to absent friends, Mr. Kramden."

★ SNAPSHOT ★

Writer Leonard Stern recalled Jackie as a generous performer, unselfish in giving laugh lines to other performers, which is often not the norm for comedians who have lived life snapping off the payoff to a two-liner in a thousand roadhouses featuring a local combo and watered liquor. They do not tend to share success with eager straight men, or squander laughs, on which they live or die.

Jackie divided the laughs because he possessed a proverbial secret weapon. With him, it was the facial library of varied expressions, which could top a gag by a twitch of a lip, add to the joke imagery by eyes which showed ignorance or innocence.

Leonard was describing a script to him once and dutifully noted that in this draft Jackie did not get many of the punch lines.

> **JACKIE:** Do I have a lot of reactions?
> **LEONARD:** Yes, you sure do.
> **JACKIE:** Then I'll be just fine.

And he was, too.

★ SNAPSHOT ★

Fans always ask, "What did the bedroom look like?"

All they ever saw was Alice or Ralph going in and out of it.

Well, I imagine the Kramden bedroom was not up to the sumptuous decor of their living room–kitchen, since Ralph believed firmly that it was dumb to decorate a room where you spent most of your time with your eyes closed.

A bedroom required a bed. Everything else was extravagance. Well, he had a bed all right. A bed big enough to support a man of some substance, and Ralph Kramden was very substantial. In fact, the weary mattress and springs sagged noticeably on his side and were high and firm on Alice's. Alice's one treasure was a well-worn green teddy bear with one eye missing, which Ralph had won for her at a carnival.

The lone window had no curtains, just a single shade with a mind of its own. Alice had a three-drawer dresser handed down from previous owners. On it was a bowl of plastic flowers (dusted daily) to add a feminine touch to the room. Ralph had a four-drawer dresser (one drawer for his Raccoon regalia). Taped to the mirror above was Ralph's Bus Driver of the Month award. There was no carpeting, but a yellow rattan mat which informed ASBURY PARK LOVES YOU! lay by the bed.

★ SNAPSHOT ★

Someone with a wry and/or sadistic sense of humor must have been responsible for the countercasting of three of motion pictures' most famous character actors for an appearance on *The Jackie Gleason Show*.

We were all nonplussed by a Murderers' Row of Charles Laughton, Edward G. Robinson, and Peter Lorre, invited to do a standup for the audience to wild applause. With laughter, it was fondly hoped. Old New Yorker Edward G. was warm and winning to the cast and crew, but the great Charles Laughton was edgy with concern, despite his decades of stage and motion picture experience, at what was probably one of his earlier appearances on live coast-to-coast television. Peter Lorre, easily tinier than any of the women in the cast, was a delightful sprite who was charming yet also kept repeating his one earnest desire, "Let's have a drink."

Nervous Charles decided that Peter had a pretty good idea there, and Jackie poured (but didn't partake). As Charles grew more expansive, and Peter more cute, Edward G. considered he didn't need liquor to stand up and wave.

It proved a very funny bit. Lorre burlesqued the Lorre character he had invented; Eddie Robinson was Rico, the master mobster; and Charles, smashed to the limits of stability, owned the house in a star turn that he could never repeat because he never could have remembered what he did. In live TV, the greatest performance in the world turned to ether in seconds.

★ SNAPSHOT ★

Fan mail is one thing, but fans you meet in person are a different matter entirely. Everyone in Show Business has had the experience of the fans who are so excited at recognizing their favorite star, they say, "Oh my gosh, you're my biggest fan!"

But then there are the ones who seem to have a hard time separating the actor's work from reality. Jackie had this experience at Toots Shor's restaurant with Peter Lorre. A very excited lady spying them came rushing to their table. Peter graciously stood up, and she exclaimed, "Are you really this short?"

"No, indeed," Jackie put in. "We only rushed out for a quick bite, so he left the rest of himself back at the hotel."

★ SNAPSHOT ★

Thanks to reruns, the fan mail still comes in today, and the major portion of it is from young people. I'm sure I'll never be out of the kitchen in many people's minds. An amusing incident happened to me on a Pan Am flight from Los Angeles to New York some years ago, when smoking was still allowed. When I boarded, I was delighted to see the seat next to mine, 4A, was empty so I could spread out and read my book without interruption from a chatty seatmate. Shortly after takeoff a young man was brought up from coach and took the seat beside me. I assumed he was a frequent flyer upgrade, but he was a quiet type fortunately and didn't initiate any conversation. As the flight progressed, the flight attendants came up from coach several times to say someone in the back would love to have my autograph. I complied happily. After about the fourth or fifth time they came up, this performance attracted the attention of my friend in 4B.

He looked up at me quizzically and said, "Why do they want your autograph?"

"I guess they've seen me on television," I replied.

"Oh, what do you do on TV?"

Not wishing to go through a lengthy explanation, I said they were probably fans of "The Honeymooners."

"You were on 'The Honeymooners'?" he asked. "What did you do?"

Patiently I said, "I played Alice Kramden."

Shocked, he exclaimed, "You played Alice Kramden?" Then he took a look at me and said, "You're old!"

Obviously this did not endear him to me, and, stuck for an answer, I returned to my book. Shortly before we started our descent to New York, he turned and informed me that he lived just outside of New York. "I'd like to invite you for dinner at my house. I have a lot of friends who'd love to meet you."

I thought to myself, Don't kiss up now. So, very sweetly I said, "No, thank you, I'd better not. . . . Who would carry my wheelchair upstairs?"

On my return to Los Angeles, again on Pan Am, again in my favorite seat, 4A, I settled in comfortably with no seatmate. Once we were airborne I saw a tall man leave his seat up front in no smoking and walk back to the center seats, where he could have a cigarette. I recognized him as the wonderful, award-winning actor Richard Harris. He sat down with his pack of cigarettes in hand and started fumbling through all his pockets for a light. He looked across at me and asked if I had a light.

"Certainly," I said, and leaned over to hand him my lighter. With that he took a long look at me and shouted, "Oh my God, you're Audrey Meadows. . . . You're gorgeous!"

"Thank you," I said. "And you're the fabulous Richard Harris." But I thought to myself, "You're old!"

A Trip to the Moon, Alice

Nineteen fifty-four was a great year for Willie Mays and his New York Giants. He won the National League batting championship, made the most spectacular catch and throw from center field in the series, and the Giants won the championship of the civilized world. New York went nuts.

But I had been coming apart in bits and pieces well before that since I had been nominated for Best Supporting Actress in a comedy by the Academy of Television Arts and Sciences. The ever-lovin' Emmy. And so had Art Carney for Best Supporting Actor in a comedy. I guess the academy had forgotten who the two of us were supporting, because they kind of excluded Jackie.

They also forgot our writers, who gave us the words to support ourselves. No, I'll take that back. The writers who also were nominated received telegrams and were advised to "be sure to watch" the awards programming. Not quite the stern notice of yesteryear, which read, "No Irish Need Apply," but ample warning that their presence was unsolicited.

I was so irate at the academy for stiffing the people who made sure that when actors opened their mouths something came out besides the National Anthem, I announced that "if they can't come to the party, then I'm not going either!" They were pals, and without them Art and I would not have been nominated.

In its collective and nearly infinite wisdom, the academy called the writers and allowed that they would be welcome at the bar during the event! Realizing that if they had been invited normally, that would have been the logical place for them to gather, I translated this into victory and, privately, guessed I would be shoulder to shoulder with them shortly after the word came from Hollywood that Vivian Vance had been selected yet once again for the honor.

Vivian was a terrific comedic actress, enjoying the extra advantage of being almost an extension of Lucille Ball, the impish and lovable clown who was probably the best this nation has ever produced. A beautiful showgirl, Lucy had stretched herself in every comedic way. Her loony getups and riotous situations with faithful Vivian by her side made you forget the alluring redhead to focus on her manic antics.

The Honeymooners and *I Love Lucy* were poles apart in how we inspired laughter and a kind of allegiance to the characters portrayed, yet they undoubtedly shared a similar audience. As Jackie would have said, "They were funny!" Neither was aimed at any particular age group or income level. It was pure family fare comedy and was accepted that way—witty and warm and, of course, clean. *The Honey-*

mooners was aired on date night, Saturday, yet young people stayed in to catch the show with older folks and kids before they went out. That wasn't unusual in the fifties. Music, for instance, wasn't just the property of the young. All ages knew the lyrics to popular ballads and had favorite singers. Everybody danced at parties and receptions, they didn't just sit deafened by the amplified guitars of the combo.

Well, I don't know what music they played at the Emmy Awards because I was involved in forcing frivolity to disguise anxiety as the presenters in Hollywood started dealing prizes. We New Yorkers made impudent comments when westerners won and cheered for our side. Art Carney and I were seated with my manager, Val Irving; Jack Philbin and Jack Hurdle; and MCA's Sonny and Leah Werblin. I had steeled myself to hear the marvelous news about Vivian Vance back in Hollywood when Jack Benny took the dais out there and announced that the winner "in New York is . . . Audrey Meadows." For a split second I thought, "Oh, my God, she won!" Then I realized it was me.

Dave Garroway was the East's award giver that night, and he was extending *My Emmy* to *me*! Amid applause, cheers, and, from the writers' wing at the bar, cheery and laudatory expletives, I gracefully knocked over my chair as I lunged at Dave and *My Emmy*. Since I had never dreamed I'd win, I had not memorized an epigram suitable for etching in marble. Art told me later I had whooped for joy on the way up, but he was obviously wrong, as I'm sure both my lips and voice box were temporarily paralyzed. But when Art won for Best Supporting Actor in a comedy, I whooped with the best of them for Our Norton.

A very nice man from the academy offered to relieve me of the statuette so they could send it to be engraved. Since

I was clutching it like a woman with a winning lottery ticket, I offered a dimpled "Thank you, no," which must have held menace in its tactfulness since he disappeared with giant steps. Several weeks later, I finally let it go so it could be engraved.

I still have the Emmy, of course, but view it more as a souvenir of great friends and great times than as some form of medal for doing your job as well as you are able.

Jackie couldn't have been happier for Art's and my awards, and never, by any sign or word, did he ever suggest he might have appreciated some professional recognition for being the star, producer, and ringmaster of the whole endeavor which had dominated the network scene for year after year. If he was hurt by being ignored by the panel while adored by the public, he hid it deep. As a matter of fact, going through old scrapbooks, I found the telegram he sent me the next morning. It read:

> **I ALWAYS KNEW I HAD THE WORLD'S**
> **GREATEST TEAM. NOW EVERYBODY ELSE**
> **DOES TOO. I AM PROUD AND DELIGHTED.**
> **JACKIE**

The Jackie Gleasons display their lights and sparkle, but they never show their wounds.

Jackie never liked anyone to be mad at him, but in our fifth season, 1956–57, he really corked me off. We were doing one-hour musical *Honeymooners*es. We had rehearsals on Friday to learn the songs for that week.

I had been married in May of 1956 and was living in Virginia. I commuted to New York Fridays. Saturday nights I hired an ambulance to get me to the airport so that I could jump in my car and be back in my house by 10:30. A call came from the office to say that Jackie was calling a rehearsal for Thursday afternoon. At that time, my husband had the mumps, which can be serious in an adult male. Not wanting to leave him, I asked to beg off, saying I could learn whatever it was on Friday, but Jackie was adamant. So I flew to New York Thursday. I reached my apartment to find a message saying rehearsal had been canceled. Naturally, I was wild. I am usually very unflappable; it takes me a long time to get boiling. But when I do, I'm not at a loss for words. I called the office and laid a few thousand on them. Unconscionably selfish, no compassion, et cetera, were the mildest.

About 4:30, Jackie was on the phone. He said, "I don't want you to be upset; it couldn't be helped. I'm sending the car for you to meet me at Toots Shor's."

"You can't send anything for me. I'm upset, and I'm going to stay upset."

"Oh come on, Aud, don't be that way, we'll talk and have dinner, et cetera, et cetera."

He was so contrite, I gave in and met him at Shor's.

Well, of course, he charmed me out of my angry mood and then became somewhat introspective. He said, "You know, Aud, life can deal you some funny hands. The world can strip you of a lot of things. They can strip you of your money, they can strip you of your reputation, but there is one thing they can never take away from you. And that's your talent."

He snapped out of his melancholy mood and said, "Come on, let's go have a great Italian dinner at Romeo Salta's." We got in Jackie's limo. He sat in the front seat with the chauffeur, since his size made it easier for him to enter and exit from there. I sat in the back, and off we went. We'd had quite a few drinks and an enormous dinner when he decided we should go to "21" for a nightcap, although it was only 7:30.

But, as we left the table, he sotto-voced, "Walk very straight," and I realized he was feeling most mellow indeed. At the "21" Club there was quite a flurry of bowing in getting us to the best table. After a few more drinks, I said I had better be getting home. As Jackie paid the check, again, out of the side of his mouth, "Walk very straight." It occurred to me that no matter how much he had imbibed, he was conscious of his public persona and did not intend to be seen lurching his way out.

Back in the limo, he said, "It's early, and you've never seen my new apartment. We'll stop by for a minute, and then the driver can take you home."

When we arrived, he showed me his extensive collection of books on ESP, paranormal psychology, and so on. These have since been donated to the University of Miami by his widow, Marilyn, and now number somewhere around two thousand works. Hypnotism always fascinated Jackie because it crossed barriers without drugs or made-up mumbo jumbo.

As I was leaving, he asked me to call him when I reached home to be sure I was all right. Talk about your mother hen—how solicitous can you be?

I said, "Jackie, I don't have your number." He guarded his private home number like the combination to the safe at Tiffany's, for reasons known only to him. But he had a solution. He would give me his number under hypnosis, and when I called, he would dismiss it from my mind. He walked me to the elevator and said, "Close your eyes, open your eyes," several times, then, "You're getting very sleepy." After much repetition, he finally gave me the number. Pretending I was mesmerized, and now entrusted with the priceless number, I slowly entered the elevator. As soon as the doors closed, I took a pen from my purse and, not being the least bit sleepy, I wrote the number down.

When I got home, dutifully I called Jackie to report I had had a most enjoyable time.

He said, "How did you get this number?"

I stammered, "I don't know, I must have had it somewhere."

He sounded so pleased, I didn't have the heart to spoil his fun. So I never told him that as a hypnotist he was a great comic actor. He may have been a scholar on hypnotism, but it was, obviously, easier to read about it than to do it.

Years later, when Jackie had moved to Florida, he became interested in the mysterious properties of the pyramidal structure. Why were pyramids a focus of the great temples and palaces of the Near East and, uncharted oceans away, found in Central and South America? Was this some unknown portent, or property, which ancients were aware of but that had been lost or forgotten? In the sixties, varied forms of pyramid-type constructions were being developed, from residences to offices. People would sit in the center and meditate. The shape was supposed to free the mind with some sort of energy. Jackie had arranged a structure for his own bed, placing it on a true north setting. He wasn't being silly about these things. He was being curious.

★ SNAPSHOT ★

A ctors are not so much superstitious as they are ritualistic. Baseball players use the same bat every day when they're on a hitting streak. Why change when your luck is running well? Some actors give silent incantations to gods who have displayed favor to them in the past. Why risk snubbing them for the next performance? That's just common sense, not any pagan voodoo.

Art Carney's dressing room was next to mine, and every show night he'd enter my room, bend over my tiny sink, turn the faucets on, and flick splashes of water, presumably at his eyes, yet the droplets would fly over both his shoulders. This one-scene playlet would be performed without words and last only a few minutes. He would then dry his fingers and depart until we met later in the midst of stage action.

Maybe his shoulders were too dry? More possibly he had had a great audience response one night after he had gone through this ritual. Whatever. But he was making sure he didn't neglect his favorite bat while he was hitting homers every Saturday.

I, on the other hand, have no such inane bargains with Fortune. I know my lines, hit my marks, remember the director's changes, and play the role as the writer wrote it.

Love, Alice

There's only one little thing.

Before my first entrance, I have this nervous gastric thing, you see, and my manager, Val Irving, waited for me to give this teeny, tiny burp, upon which he would say, "Now we'll have a good show."

It used to be an unladylike belch, but I don't do that anymore.

If there comes a time I can't burp, I'm going to wash my hands and throw the water drops over my shoulders.

Couldn't hurt, right?

Honeymooners
for Always

I f the august Emmy board was reticent about acknowledg-
ing showman Jackie's gifts, the Buick division of General
Motors was not, signing him (and us) for 1955 and beyond.
When the contract was finally assembled and cross-
checked by platoons of lawyers, Jackie had gained the high-
est salary and supplemental income since the invention of
entertainment.

The Honeymooners was to be an 8:30 to 9:00 filmed show
on Saturday night preceded by a half hour called *Stage
Show*, produced by Jackie and featuring Tommy and Jimmy
Dorsey's bands. The sponsor's price for two years was $11
million!

Now I realize that today it is difficult to sign a left-
handed shortstop for that kind of money, but in 1955 it was
absolutely stupendous. Naturally, Jackie had to pay all the
talent from this sum, as well as production costs, but it was

far, far over the full-hour costs of the previous *Jackie Glea-son Show*. This was not the pinnacle of Show Business. It was Mt. Everest looking down at the little pinnacles.

Tremendous publicity followed for all of us. I believe it was *TV Guide* that did the story on Art and me, calling us "the Million Dollar Babies." How wrong they were. Jackie Gleason Enterprises would never be that charitable, but it made good copy.

Two things occurred almost immediately to prove to me it wasn't a dream. They were:

1. My grocery bill inherited an additional tier of prices of items I had not purchased, with no receipts enclosed.
2. My garage parking rent doubled overnight.

I called the grocery store to inform them if they wanted the bill paid, they would have to send me the receipts, as they had always done in the past. The satisfaction I got was in the form of a question—"You mean you see your own bills, Miss Meadows? We thought you had a business manager."

I asked my hairdresser when the garage had upped the monthly bill, since he parked there also. He said, "It hasn't changed. There's still a big sign out front with the monthly charge on it." Since I had always used their pickup and delivery service, I thought it would be wise to drive over there with my bill in hand. Red faces all around, as I explained that they should not believe everything they read in the press. Having convinced both parties of their arithmetic errors, I resumed wary relationships based on previous costs for services.

With Buick coming on board as our sponsor, new contracts had to be negotiated. Earlier in this saga, I told you about the rigorous contest of wills with Bullets Durgom and MCA versus Little Audrey. This time I faced much the same players.

Like any woman whose concern for her livelihood and future is viewed as an impediment to commerce and progress by lawyers who have a client who has told them so, I realized that now was the time I needed to have my own lawyers. Both my brothers were attorneys, and I have depended all my life on their good advice. Fortunately, my brother Ed was living in New York, so he was my adviser and counsel throughout this tense period, working with my theatrical attorney, the well-known Mortimer Becker. Morty is not only a great lawyer but a master at negotiation. All his star clients have done well through the years thanks to his ability. He also has been the lawyer for our AFTRA union for many years. He was, and still is, my lawyer and a treasured friend. We have been through a lot together.

So the contest began. The contract was for two years, thirty-nine weeks each year. As time and negotiations went on, I would dream up something else I thought should be included. I often called Ed at a late hour to suggest a new rider which I thought would be fulfilling. He would patiently (or impatiently) explain to me that I couldn't ask for that because of this or that reason. Or "On what basis do you think you can ask for that?" he would ask grimly. My answer was always "Girls' rules." These two words have worked very well with me. They can win a lot of arguments in marriage too.

Weeks and months went by, and the sticking point seemed to be the residual payments. Both Morty and Ed assured me I had gotten more riders into the contract than had ever appeared in a single document outside of a congressional pork barrel bill. It was sprouting contractual twigs and branches, and the opposition had become stubborn going for surly. I had urged Art Carney to get his own lawyer and seek a more favorable residual agreement for himself.

I said, "Artie, you're standing in my way. You're billed over me, and salaried over me, and you rate the very top."

Art was, and is, a sweetheart in addition to being a truly great actor (remember, he took the Oscar in 1974 for Best Actor in *Harry and Tonto*). Yet offstage Art was far from being an extrovert. He wasn't a timid man, but he was humble, in that he didn't claim the privileges he richly deserved. My urging for him to get legal representation to speak up strongly on the residual issue didn't go anywhere. Art accepted the standard (at that time) five-year term for residuals. I did not, although my brother Ed told me that I was so far out in left field I could eat hot dogs in the bleachers.

During this period, we had all received the Buicks of our choice as part of the deal. My choice was a bright lipstick red convertible with a white top, wire wheels, and white sidewall tires. It was gorgeous! I went tooling around all over New York. That car brought me so much luck. I have had a red car ever since, no matter what make. So I'm a little superstitious, it can't hurt. I gave Jackie and some friends a ride in it one day. It must have been Jackie's thin period because he was in the backseat. As I was maneuvering in the city traffic, I heard him whisper, "Watch this, I'll get her crazy. Aud," he asked loudly, "why didn't you get the big model like mine?"

"Jackie Gleason, I heard you, and this model is exactly the same as yours."

Meanwhile, the contract negotiations were at a temporary stalemate when my phone rang one day. It was Jack

Philbin telling me that all the head honchos at Buick were coming to New York and wanted to meet the cast at dinner. He was very effusive and chatty, unlike his usual calls. Just before he hung up, he said as a throwaway, "Oh, by the way, when you come for dinner, don't mention that you haven't signed your contract. They're not interested in that."

"I won't, of course," I replied.

I hung up and thought, That was strange! Then it hit me, and I danced all around the room. I dialed my brother and screamed, "Tell Morty we don't have to give in on the residuals." He thought he was going to hear some more "girls' rules" nonsense. But I repeated Philbin's conversation, and he understood my delight.

It meant that Buick had bought *The Honeymooners*, not Jackie Gleason alone, and, obviously, Jackie's deal was to deliver Art and Joyce and me as a package. Of course, Jack Philbin didn't want Buick to know I was the only one not signed. Philbin never knew how important that call was to me, and he won't unless he reads it here.

The last meeting on my contract closely resembled a Lions versus Christians contest. Since I was a minister's daughter, my side was not among the lions. The opposition surrounding the table counted eleven lawyers set to knock my two guys into the cheap seats. We had short odds, but our hearts were pure. It had been raining hard outside, so when Morty Becker and my brother walked in, they were outfitted from head to toe in raingear. Jack Philbin was in a sardonic mood. "Take a look at their feet, fellows," he snorted, noting the thick rubbers on their shoes. "We're going to get screwed today!"

So they agreed that I would get residuals on my participation in *The Honeymooners* in perpetuity for the reruns. Naturally, I never dreamed, nor did anyone else, that the show would go on, and on, and on. Like Ralph Kramden, we backed a dark horse but unlike Ralph, we pegged a winner. Has to happen happy sometime, right?

With all contracts, riders have to be initialed. I was initialing away when I came to the morals clause. This was explicit enough to be banned from most libraries. I had to acknowledge that if I performed any of these practices and it came to public attention, the contract was voided. If I had done 10 percent of what was listed, I would have been in a nut ward or an isolation cell. The only thing left out was if you did it with a goat on Fifth Avenue. But all the contracts had to match, so I initialed that too.

Knowing if there were any additions or alterations to a contract, they would have to be initialed by the parties, and wanting Jackie to know I was pleased, I drew a big heart in the margin with a message inside, "J.G. loves A.M.," for him to initial.

Years later, I ran into Jackie on Fifty-second Street, and he said, "Come on, I'll buy you a drink." So into "21" we went, and we reminisced about old times.

During the conversation he said, "Aud, are you still getting paid for *The Honeymooners*?" When I answered, "Yes," he said, "I never figured out quite how you managed that."

Thank you, Morty. Thank you, Ed.

As I have earlier reported, the 1955–56 season of half-hour *Honeymooners*es became the show's unique mark in television entertainment history and a kind of perpetually living heritage. These were the segments which have been screened over and over on channels throughout the nation and are still on schedule. WPIX-TV in New York City actually ran them for twenty-five years straight. Somehow, the show seemed to find a younger audience each year while keeping the one that was already watching. I think the market research guys must have broken their computers trying to figure the cost per viewer, demographics, and consumer loyalty of an audience that wouldn't go away for more than a quarter of a century and knew the plots so well they could have cued the actors.

What the public didn't know was the incredible record set by Jackie Gleason for that season. We did thirty-nine half hour shows in just under twenty weeks. We filmed two shows a week. That had never been done before and has never been done since. We had Monday off waiting for the script; Tuesday we went to the theatre and did the show. We had Wednesday and Thursday off, and Friday we went to the theatre again for another show. We were so far ahead about the eighth or tenth week that Jackie called us in and said, "Do you want to take a break for a week or so and then come back to do the rest?" and we all agreed. Today you work five full days to do a half-hour comedy. Working with Jackie was the greatest training in the world. The only drawback to this style was how hard it was to get back in the habit of rehearsals again in the years following. When I did specials with Sid Caesar, his style was thorough rehearsals for two weeks before going into the theatre to tape the shows. Sid is a comedy genius, unsurpassed to this day.

Jackie, with his photographic memory, was always a one-read rehearsal. That, of course, let him take liberties with dialogue and movements since he could usually (not always) play some improvisational games and get back to the story line within the time allotted to the script. Stanley Poss, our associate producer and stage manager, would kneel in front of a camera giving Jackie the thirty- or forty-five-second sign, and Jackie could mentally make the cut and finish on the nose.

Jackie was professional to his fingertips, and his sensitivity to other actors was phenomenal. I recall what he told me one time when he was doing a guest appearance on a dramatic show. A first reading is a time of trial and torment for the actor; everyone feels insecure. All the actors were sitting around the table for their first reading of the script. Then the producer came in and started whispering to the director.

"I could feel the other actors growing uneasy," Jackie recalled, "so I stood it for about two minutes, then I bellowed, 'What are you whispering about?'" When Jackie bellowed, his voice could reach the last row in the balcony.

The flustered producer said, "Keep going, we're just discussing a problem with the set design."

"Oh," said Jackie. "You're whispering so you won't hurt the set's feelings, are you? Well, speak up, the set won't mind. Don't you know when you whisper, you make every actor at this table feel guilty? Actors think you're talking about them, and their ever-present insecurity takes over. Why don't you whisper to the set after we leave, and let's get on with the show, as they say?"

Even though I had worked with Jackie going on four years at this time, I was still not aware of his grasp of other arcane arts. I happened to walk in on him at the Park Sheraton headquarters one day to find him sitting up on a high stool, cutting and editing *Honeymooners* film as professionally as a film editor in Hollywood, which he revealed is where he had learned the skill. Restless in the small parts of his five movies, he had wandered around the lot. Strolling along one day, he heard whirring sounds coming from an open door. He approached to find it was the editing room. From then on, when he wasn't working he made his

Love, Alice

way there and learned the techniques of transferring the acting on the set into the film product.

"Anything and everything you can learn about this business is never lost," he instructed. "It will come in handy someday."

Just maybe this dyed-in-the-wool New Yorker did have a secret wish to go back to Hollywood and show those West Coast yahoos what they'd missed when they cast him in roles that did not allow him to display his range of talents. I say this because there was some pressure to move *The Honeymooners* to Los Angeles following its resounding success. Whether it was more network or more sponsor, I don't know, but Jackie put it up to the cast and received a unanimous "No!" in response. We stayed in Manhattan. If he was the dictator, as some people insist he was, Jackie wouldn't have asked for any opinion but his own, and the Kramdens would have begun sporting California tans. Even Ed Norton, in the depths of the sewer.

About this time, Bob and Ray asked me to join them on their show if I had the time. I had the time and was having a ball sitting in for half a dozen panel shows which used comedy twists in weeknight Q and A and game-type shows, which were then all the fad. Since there was nothing in my eleven-lawyer contract to stop me, and it didn't interfere with *The Honeymooners*, I was delighted to work with Bob Elliott and Ray Goulding again.

Bullets Durgom was unhappy enough to have me in house arrest. Words were spoken between us. An impasse was reached. Jackie was summoned to rule from on high.

"Why do you want to do this, Aud?" he asked.

"Because when I needed a job, they took me on when they didn't have to," I said. "Now they need me."

"That's the best reason I know," said Jackie. "I'll be

watching the show if it doesn't run into the cocktail hour. Leave Alice here. Go be Audrey."

Personnel directors, please note that management and labor responsibilities are simplified in the Gleason manual.

The fifties was a time when audiences fell in love with *The Honeymooners* and with TV game and panel shows. And you could hardly flip a channel without catching me on thirty-minute entertainments like *The Name's the Same*, *Keep Talking* (a team effort at a sport I'm good at), *I'll Buy That!* hosted by Mike Wallace (pre-pre *60 Minutes*), and *Masquerade Party*, with Faye Emerson, Bert Parks, and Lee Bowman.

Most weren't for big money prizes, just a chance to catch Show Biz personalities revealing they can be as smart or as dumb as the viewers, while being entertaining doing it.

What's Going On? was such a show and had a lively run each week, with one of the panel being sent to an unlikely place anywhere in the country to do unlikely things and then stump the other panelists on where he or she had been and what he or she had done. One week I was sent to Princeton to be in the famous Princeton Triangle Show. But the best was when our devious producer sent me all the way to the Chicago Federal Reserve Bank to burn a million dollars of perfectly legal bills which had become too threadbare for public usage.

So, class, the Feds took me down to the dungeons of the bank and showed me how you could warm yourself beside the most expensive fire in Chicago since Mrs. O'Leary's cow kicked over the lantern.

But you don't just heave fluttering bills in the general direction of the flickering grate of the fireplace. No indeed. First, they had a machine which sliced up the greenbacks so they would not make tasteful samples for dungeon shoppers. Then there was this other machine which punctured holes into all the slices. Only then did they bundle this wealthy garbage and let Audrey get her hands on it. And Audrey, with a tear in her eye, heaved bricks of filthy lucre into a blazing (and extremely well guarded) furnace.

The following week, no one on the show guessed what had gone on with me, since this escapade was guaranteed to stump the panel.

While this has nothing to do with "The Honeymooners," I offer it as an educational tidbit, in case you didn't know what happened to the old scrungy bills you've been slaving your life away to get.

I never did count how many shows I was on, but it was fun, and I did so many guest shots on my own time during the week that I met myself coming and going. Bullets Durgom, of course, made mad noises about my appearing on other shows and other networks, but Jackie realized I was so identified with *The Honeymooners*, I was like a walking, talking advertisement for the show, so he said, "Go, enjoy!" I did.

Edward R. Murrow evidently thought that I was on TV more than the law should allow and decided it might be nice if his cameras and crew visited my sister and me in our apartment on his mega-rated *Person to Person* show to see how we really lived.

We thought this would be a snap, until we realized the world was coming into our nice, cozy apartment and we had a rather large glitch to face. They were expecting to film two successful actresses in their glamorous Manhattan apartment. How to tell them there would be no furniture in the living room? My sister was planning to get married shortly, and I had decided to redecorate. Everything new had been ordered, and my decorator had suggested it would be easier if I moved all the old stuff out, so we could move all the new pieces into a fresh room. The moving men had come the day before the Murrow producers arrived. I only left the carpeting and one wing chair because they didn't fit on the truck. Rather than show our embarrassment, we decided to act as if this was a perfectly normal way to live. But you can imagine the shock on the faces of Murrow's producers, Jesse Zousmer and John A. Aaron, when we opened the door to usher them in. Jesse sat in the big chair; the rest of us sat on chairs we brought in from the dining room.

When the situation had been explained to him, he hopefully asked when the new furniture was arriving.

I replied, "Not only will it not arrive in time for the show, but the moving man will arrive any minute to take away the chair you're sitting on." A call went through to Ed Murrow, who was highly amused, and they decided to open the show with us both out on the terrace, which had furniture. We did borrow a couch from a very accommodating neighbor for the broadcast.

They interviewed us at great length but wouldn't give us a clue as to what questions would be asked on air. Show day arrived, and the crew came to set up the equipment, cameras, et cetera.

Several hours before the show, we were wired for sound. This consists of a battery pack placed under your dress in the back and the wire brought around and up to the front, where the microphone could be clipped. It never occurred to us that from that moment on anyone in the studio at CBS could listen in on our conversations, or trips to the bathroom.

The show went off with a sparkle, and since we still had our microphones on and could talk to Murrow back at the studio, we invited him and his staff for drinks and buffet.

Ed Murrow was a very handsome man and a fascinating conversationalist. We were spellbound by his stories about London during the war. His whole team was great, and we sat around on the floor talking for hours.

The next time I saw Jackie, he greeted me with sympathetic noises and said, "We're going to pass the hat around for you, Aud, so you can buy some furniture!"

I'm not sure whether it was the drinks, or the buffet, or the show he liked, but shortly after I was asked to substitute for Ed Murrow when he went on vacation. Would you say no? No, you wouldn't. Not when that tanned and gorgeous man with the muscles in his throat, who made "This is London calling" a song of love to the women of America in World War II, asked you to do it.

I was given my choice of whom I wished to interview, so I chose Broadway producer Josh Logan and his wife, actress Nedda Harrigan, and the sports columnist Jimmy Cannon. It was great being on the other side this time. They were just as eager to find out what questions I would ask them as I had been, and they got the same answer—fat chance! Who was I to tamper with the format of the hottest show in town?

After Murrow saw the very nice review I received in *Variety* (the show business bible), he sent me the following wire:

> **I THINK EVERYONE IN THE STUDIO AND PROBA-BLY THE COUNTRY WAS SORRY YOU WEREN'T SITTING IN THE CHAIR LAST FRIDAY NIGHT. AGAIN MANY THANKS.**
>
> **REGARDS—ED MURROW**

Our 1955–56 show year was remarkable for two significant reasons, one of which we didn't suspect at the time.

First was the Electronicam filming of the show, which preserved this particular season for infinity on the airwaves. The second and shocking development was Jackie's feeling that our script material was becoming perilously thin. He knew the acting was still good, but he wanted somehow to stretch *The Honeymooners*, find a legitimate reason to get the characters out of the apartment and still keep them believable.

Privately, some of us had noticed that the leadoff position of the Dorsey Brothers in our Buick one-hour show had not been the best thing to happen to us. They weren't pulling a good rating. For three prior years, NBC had thrown every star in the business against us—Fred Allen, Tallulah Bankhead, Jimmy Durante—and still they could not shake our position. The year before they had made a big-money offer to me to go with NBC. However, I was aware of the fact that they didn't have a project in mind for me; it was simply a ploy to weaken the chemistry Jackie had going in *The Honeymooners,* and I was very happy where I was.

So NBC decided to hit us with a pillow instead of a rock. They gave warm, gentle, relaxed Perry Como his own musical feature. *The Perry Como Show* was slotted opposite *Stage Show,* and NBC came up with a winner. Perry had a pleasant, tuneful one-hour show. With the Dorsey Brothers' half hour as our lead-in, much of the audience just stayed with Perry for the hour instead of changing to *The Honeymooners*. It was a competition between one musical presentation and another, and Como's offering was preferred to the Dorseys'. He was topping them handily in the ratings. Jackie felt that if *The Honeymooners* had kicked off the hour, we would have retained our loyal audience. We still were up among the nation's top shows but not the runaway leader of Saturday night.

So he decided to return to doing a one-hour show—and to cancel the Buick deal and his huge new contract!

His judgment that the scripts had gone soft was not apparent to the rest of us and certainly has not been borne out by the popularity of that material shown over and over for forty years, in which new generations have taken the Kramden carnival to their hearts. Out in Michigan, the Buick executives were aghast—they could not understand a star giving up a hit show, to say nothing of a lucrative contract.

CBS was as much in shock at Jackie's decision as Buick had been. But sponsors were waiting in line to buy into the musical *Honeymooners*. So, CBS's initial shock turned into delight to have the Great One back with a full hour. Jackie, the perfectionist, had his way. And, awaaay we went!

So the 1956–57 season we were back to the one-hour *Honeymooners,* but this time in musical form. The musical shows were right up my alley since I had done so many musicals in summer stock in Chicago, Detroit, Louisville, New Jersey, pick-a-city.

The story line had Ralph entering the fictional Flaky Waky contest and winning a trip to Europe for the four of us. So it was decided that *The Honeymooners* would go musical for the hour with ten colorful trips to Europe, celebrated by a complete musical comedy confected each week by the incredible team of Jerry Bresler and Lyn Duddy. Try to write *Hello, Dolly!* every week, or even *The PTA Follies.* Impossible, of course, but it happened. Doing musicals made it necessary for us to rehearse on Fridays to learn the songs. There were usually six to eight new songs in each show. Of course, came the Friday rehearsal when Jackie thought the show highlighting a vacation in Norway was not up to standard.

So help me, Jerry and Lyn wrote new songs in hours, and June Taylor staged new dances. New costumes and sets appeared, and there we were in Ireland. From glaciers to Galway, in one day, with all of us reading a TelePrompTer for the lyrics.

After five prior years on Arthur Godfrey's show, described by Jerry Bresler as "torture and more torture," the music and lyrics duo were overjoyed to be part of our show. Both viewed Jackie as a gentleman who couldn't have been nicer to them following their previous experience.

Hired on a Monday, they were expected to prepare a full-scale musical production by that Saturday. And, of course, they did. Signed for seven more shows, they invented and confected songs for the millions that had pace, charm, and gusto. I particularly recall our "England" production, which had two great numbers—"Everything Stops for Tea" and "I Tyke to You and You Tyke to Me"— that would have been showstoppers on Broadway. Their song "Hospitality" was recorded by the Sun Tones for jukeboxes everywhere.

In another spot for another show, they put together the titles of the songs recorded by Bing Crosby and composed a single song wedding all sixty-eight titles. Bing was so enamored by the feat that he recorded a sixty-ninth song— Jerry and Lyn's amalgamation of his recorded work.

Jackie had certain curious requests for numbers, like a song on a rooftop, or in a cellar, or about a mouse. Presumably, the mouse could be on a rooftop or in a cellar, but I don't recall any rodent rhapsody, so either they talked Jackie out of the idea or he forgot it.

They considered that Jackie had talent as big as an iceberg, "but you only saw the tip," according to Jerry. "He had a depth of stage skill and knowledge that few ever discovered because he used it so naturally." The Gleason years were a pinnacle for Lyn and Jerry.

The 1956–57 season flew by. I don't remember when we learned, or who told us, that that would be the last year of the show, but our reactions were not significant in any way. No shock or dismay. We were all young and ready to move on with our lives and careers. After the last show, the four of us gathered in Jackie's dressing room and had a marvelous gabfest about how we'd been together for five years bringing Ralph and Alice, Norton and Trixie to life, so that the characters had become shadow personalities of each of us. No tears, no groans. It didn't seem possible that five years had gone by. It was more like going to a party every week. There were no toasts, no banquet, just kisses and hugs, as was the rule at the close of any happy troupe. In Show Business, you never really say good-bye, because you're not leaving the business, just changing hats, and we'd all be running into each other again very soon.

I've always felt that every closing is an opening to something else.

Art Carney appeared on many TV dramatic shows, proving once again that a skilled comic actor is an actor first, then a comic, and he would alternate between Broadway theatre and television and, finally, Hollywood and motion pictures. Art can do it all in the theatre. He can be dignified or zany, sensitive or rowdy, courageous or pathetic. He has played many roles in his career, but he recalls, "When Norton entered the room, you always knew something was going to happen."

Joyce Randolph began a family and was nothing like Trixie, the former burlesque stripper wed to Ed Norton, the sewer man. We recently had a ball when we went to Disney World together and were cheered by all the youngsters who recognized us from our constant reruns.

After *The Honeymooners,* I played everything—*Alfred Hitchcock Presents, Kraft Television Theatre, Wagon Train, Checkmate,* and so on, with all stops in between plus motion pictures. But in 1960, I met the love of my life, Robert F. Six, and we were married the next year. Bob was the president of Continental Airlines, which was then headquartered in Denver; it moved to Los Angeles in 1963. I was very much in love for twenty-five years, and I wanted to be with my husband just as much as I could. And I was until Bob died in 1986. I treasure every moment we shared.

★ SNAPSHOT ★

Jackie was not a whiz on his monologues opening *The Jackie Gleason Show*. The setup lines threw him off. Jackie Gleason would be completely out of character if he prefaced a gag with "A funny thing happened to me in the supermarket the other day . . ." because the audience would disbelieve immediately that a brassy Broadway type like himself had ever been near a supermarket. He said, "They'll know I'm lying."

Finally, he hired a monologist writer, Selma Diamond, a veteran gag specialist from the days of the great Goodman Ace on radio, who later would go before the camera as the whiny, waspish bailiff of TV's *Night Court*.

Everything Selma said sounded funny. It seemed her adenoids were at war with the rest of her throat, giving a kind of strange singsong tone to her choppy, metered rendition of very common occurrences. She came across as a woman who faced a world which not only didn't appreciate her but was having a hard time even understanding her.

I don't know whether her gags were any more clever than the other writers', but she certainly made Jackie feel he was getting a jump on his jokes rather than collapsing into them. "This is my Valhalla," he caroled at his new approach. "I've finally licked it."

A happy man is a jolly man. He can make everybody laugh.

★ SNAPSHOT ★

One of the greatest thrills in my career was working with Alfred Hitchcock. He had me come to California to do a dramatic role on his television show, *Alfred Hitchcock Presents*. The episode was called "Mr Bixby and the Colonel's Coat," which later won an award.

Each day I went to the studio for wardrobe fittings, he either invited me for lunch or for tea. And each time I thought, "Now he will discuss the role with me." I was wrong; we talked of nothing but books.

He gave very little direction, and when he did, he would walk the actor away from the crew so no one could hear what he was saying.

I had a breakfast scene, during which I had to take a bite of toast and jam. On a second take, the prop man had to replace the toast. I was not used to getting up at five in the morning, and by the time we shot the scene, I was very hungry. Mr Hitchcock noticed that I was nervously consuming all the toast and jam in between takes. He dryly said to me, "Miss Meadows, we can add eggs and bacon to the scene if you're still hungry."

I swallowed and smiled. No one did verbal fencing with Alfred Hitchcock. No one.

I'm the King
of the Castle

Jackie showed he was more than a wild-eyed Brooklyn bus driver when he made three movies in the early sixties, creating exceptional roles in *Gigot* and *Requiem for a Heavyweight,* and meriting an Academy Award nomination for Best Supporting Actor as Minnesota Fats in *The Hustler.*

He also relocated *The Jackie Gleason Show* to Miami at this time.

An enterprising Miami press agent, Hank Meyer, played the Lorelei to lure Jackie and Company to sunny Miami. As publicist for Miami, he had sold the city on Jackie and his show as a spectacular tourist attraction. What really sold Our Jackie was the fact that he had become enamored of golf. In Florida, he would never run out of golf courses to correct his slice and better his putting.

The city built a huge auditorium for Jackie with the latest technical innovations, enabling the show to switch from black and white to color. The shows, and Jackie himself, became a tourist attraction. He married again, and he played days of golf.

While Jackie enjoyed his game of golf, he always liked a little edge, if he could find it. Phil Cuoco told me about a manic one he used in Florida. It seemed that perennial golf partner–producer Jack Philbin had a doctor's appointment for a checkup one afternoon when Jackie was particularly anxious to separate two "pigeons" (friends from New York) from their cash in a friendly foursome. Learning that Philbin had been given a specimen jar to bring a urine sample as part of the examination, Jackie not only persuaded Philbin to postpone his visit but devised a scheme which would give the Gleason-Philbin end of the foursome the psychological advantage, even if they were behind on the ninth hole.

The empty specimen jar was filled with yellow Gatorade, and the sting was on.

The "pigeons" were flying at the end of nine. Producer Philbin, turning actor, stated he had to stop the match due to a doctor's appointment for a test for sugar. Jackie gave a Class A bellow, grabbed the specimen bottle, removed the cap, and chugalugged all the Gatorade as the pigeons quailed.

"Forget the doctor's visit, Philbin," Gleason snapped. "I can't find any sugar in there." The visitors, alarmed and unwell, lost all focus on their game, and the two Jacks went on to victory.

This is a happy ending?

I don't know, but I'm sure the losers told everybody back in Manhattan that Jackie had gone bananas from the heat down south, and they saved more money getting free drinks to tell the story than the two Jacks won on the match.

But Jackie became more restless, more lonely in Miami. Miami was not New York.

He drove about at night a lot, called all-night disc jockeys to chat about things he would have been hooted down for by the gang at "21," Toots Shor's, Jimmy Ryan's, or Joe & Rose's in Manhattan. But in Miami he was deferred to and treated like a trophy rather than a regular guy. Every time he went out in the daytime, he was mobbed like a Hollywood star. Often, after a conversation with a late-night DJ, he'd have to hurry out before a crowd gathered at the station.

He was a big frog in a small pond. But he missed the big pond, where he could be just one big frog among a lot of other wild, unpredictable, talented, cosmopolitan geniuses and goofies. He was homesick.

Jackie only agreed to be in Florida for one year and signed his contract to that effect. The first and second year he did a variety show with name guests such as Lucille Ball and Milton Berle, since he had stated he was never going to do "The Honeymooners" again.

Sometime during a meeting in the second year, show writer Walter Stone brought up an idea for "The Honeymooners."

Jackie said, "We can't do it, we don't have the set, the furniture, or the props."

A hand was raised, and his man Friday, the ever faithful Phil Cuoco, said, "Yes, we do."

Jackie, stunned, said, "What are you saying?"

Phil replied, "I packed the entire set back in New York and put it on the train, Boss, and stored it here in Miami."

Although I had seen Jackie from time to time, I had not seen him after he moved to Florida in 1964, so I was very surprised to receive a phone call from him in '66. Bob and

I were in New York, and I was appearing on a panel show when the stage manager said there was a call for me on the backstage phone. Puzzled as to who could have tracked me down at the theatre, I went to the phone to hear the familiar voice of the Great One. Jackie said he was planning to do a special, a musical version of the "Adoption" script. This, as I've explained before, was one of the most powerful and touching hour shows that we had done in the fifties. Art was available, and Jackie just needed to know if I would do it. I said, "Yes," almost before he finished the sentence. Then he threw in the hook—we would rehearse it the week between Christmas and New Year's and tape it New Year's Eve.

Fortunately, Bob and I were not sentimental about New Year's Eve. How many forced-fun parties can you go to over the years? Off I went to Miami, and the show was a great success. Lyn Duddy and Jerry Bresler again wrote the songs to fit the characters and situations. We watched the replay in Jackie's office. He was riding high, so happy. I realized that these were his favorite characters of all the many he had created.

He kept saying, "Aud, you have to come back; you are Alice, you know it!" Over and over, he wouldn't give it up. He made it very hard to resist. But I didn't have to think it over.

I had seen too many marriages break up under the pressure of dual careers, with husbands and wives trying to clear their schedules so they could be together for a day or two between business trips or client meetings or camera days. I had found happiness with the greatest man I've ever met, and I had vowed never to risk our marriage by chasing roles which would shine on a résumé but would be cold comfort if I found myself reading them all alone.

Bob didn't make this rule for me. He wasn't that kind of a guy. Aside from making several movies in Los Angeles, it was my idea, and it was, for me, one of the best I've ever made. Our life together was a jewel. We traveled all over the nation and the world together. I became absorbed in the business of the airline down to designing the interiors of our DC-10s and 747s.

As well as working in Los Angeles doing guest shots on TV, and in between Bob's business trips, I had a wonderful five years starting in 1981 with Ted Knight as a recurring character on *Too Close for Comfort*. The producer, Arne Sultan (famous for *Get Smart* and many other hit shows), was a real pal. He would never schedule my shows if they interfered with my traveling with Bob. Bless you, Arne.

So here was Jackie trying to talk me into working in Miami. Finally, we all went to dinner, with a genuine reason to celebrate New Year's Eve. I had told Bob I would call him at midnight Miami time, which would be 9:00 P.M. in Los Angeles. Art's wife, Jean, was with him, and, with such old and dear friends, there was much hilarity around the table. Yet I kept sneaking looks at my watch to check the time for my call. Jackie was in prime form, holding court, so a few minutes before midnight, I quietly got up from the table, saying I was going to the ladies' room. As I passed Jackie, without missing a beat in midsentence, he said, "You're not going to the ladies' room, you're going to call Bob." Maybe the man was either a psychic or a very good guesser.

It wasn't too long after this that I received a call from Jack Philbin asking me for a meeting. When we met, he asked me if I could give them six or seven dates that I could work in Miami since they now knew Bob had a very busy travel schedule I would have to work around. That's the airline business. On our second meeting, I gave Jack the dates, and he seemed very pleased, but he said, "To play it safe, you better give us eleven or twelve available weeks."

I hated to go back to Bob again, but I managed to work it out. The third meeting I should have smelled it coming.

Audrey Meadows

"That's great, Aud," said Philbin, "but, you know, to protect ourselves . . ."

I stopped him in midsentence and said, "Jack, level with me. You really have thirty-nine weeks, don't you?" He looked very chagrined, and I continued, "There is no way I would leave Bob for thirty-nine weeks to be in Miami. We've always been friends, so let's stay friends and you get someone else."

He blanched and choked out, "How are we going to get someone else?"

I said, "The same way you got me. You'll find the right actress."

They got Sheila MacRae for Alice and Jane Kean for Trixie, and the Kramdens had a second life. They redid the musical trips we had done in New York the last year, and they held up well. I ran into Sheila at Danny's Hideaway (another popular Manhattan watering hole) one night before they started.

She moaned, "Jackie wants me to dye my hair red."

I said, "Pay no attention, that's only because I have red hair and our shows were in black and white. Wear a red wig the first couple of shows and gradually lighten it to your color. No one will notice the difference."

George Petrie, "The Honeymooners" ' prime character actor, told me just this year that when he rejoined the cast in Miami, he asked why I wasn't doing Alice.

Somebody told him, "She asked for too much money." That's Show Business! Money was never discussed. Just thought I'd set the record straight. Jackie had a good run of the show in Miami for several years, but eventually the curtain does have to come down.

I've been told that when the management of the New York Giants football team decides to cut players, the period is known as the Time of the Turk, presumably because the fictitious Turk is a ruthless executioner with a wicked scimitar to assist the cutting. Well, the Turk really got in his slashes in the 1970–71 TV season.

The Jackie Gleason Show was axed. And Jackie was in good company. Red Skelton's long-running show was scrubbed. Two veterans walked the plank. It seemed that market research had fallen in love with demographics, and their random samples told them that while enormous numbers of people were watching the shows and enjoying them, they weren't the right age group for sponsors, who were enamored with youth, youth, youth. The fact that youth couldn't afford to buy Buicks and middle-aged people could didn't fit into the equation somehow. It wasn't until years later (the graying of America) that sponsors aimed their sales messages at those who could afford to buy high-ticket items.

I can't recall who succeeded Gleason and Skelton. Perhaps the computer loved the replacements, but, evidently, the public did not.

Surprisingly, it was the American Broadcasting Company, not Mother CBS, who called us back for a twenty-fifth anniversary special in 1976 with Jane Kean as Trixie. And for a Christmas special in 1977 and a Valentine's Day special the next year. The shows were vintage "Honeymooners," the ratings excellent, and we all had a ball. By this time, Continental was flying Los Angeles to Miami. So when Jackie playfully growled at me, "How come you can get here now, when you couldn't be in the show before?" I let him know: "Because Continental didn't fly here then."

In 1976, I flew to Miami for rehearsals. Jane Kean and I were staying at the Diplomat and were picked up by limo every day to drive to Jackie's home at the Country Club at

Lauderhill. The first day after the hugs and kisses were out of the way, we sat around a big table to read through the script. Not having seen Jackie or Art in quite a few years, I had a hard time not noticing some changes. Art now had a hearing aid, and his once lean, tight body had acquired a comfortable paunch. With our heads down reading the script, I realized that Jackie's speech sounded different. As I listened more, it occurred to me that he had probably acquired false teeth. Then I found it hard not to laugh as I wondered what they must have been thinking about me. "Jeez, she's not as thin as she was," or worse.

We did one of the specials in Atlantic City and also played five nights at Resorts International Hotel Casino Theatre. I drove down from New York, checked into the hotel, and, while I was unpacking and getting settled, the phone rang. It was Jack Philbin. "Can you come down and meet me in the casino as soon as possible?"

I said, "Of course."

When I met him he said, "You've got to help me out. Jackie is playing blackjack, he's won a lot of money, and he's drinking and he'll lose it all back."

"What can I do?"

He said, "Go over and take a seat next to him. Keep taking some of his money!"

"Jack, I can't do that, the dealer will shoot me."

"No, he won't. Just ask Jackie to stake you," he said cavalierly.

So, like an idiot, I went over and took a seat next to Jackie, and, to my horror, saw that it was a hundred-dollar table. I like to play blackjack but never for a hundred dollars a chip. I'm a very chintzy gambler.

Nervously I said, "Jackie, can I play along with you?"

"Sure, Aud" was his reply.

And he pushed over a pile of chips from his large stacks. I played a few hands and, miracle of miracles, kept winning. I watched him out of the corner of my eye, and each time he reached for his drink, I grabbed a handful of his chips and put them in my purse. This was very embarrassing. When I decided I had taken enough, a couple of thousand, I left the table, walked over to Philbin, and emptied my purse in his pockets. He thanked me and said Jackie would never remember.

The next day at rehearsal, Jackie asked, "Aud, what did you do with my money?"

I said, "I gave it to Philbin."

Never remember, huh? Never underestimate the mark, booze or no booze. Jackie was pleased, but somewhere in New Jersey that dealer is regaling friends with a description of the bimbo actress who is really a crook. Fortunately, Jackie's wife Marilyn arrived the next day, so I no longer had to play nursemaid, or fast fingers, at the casino.

The night we opened in the Casino Theatre, the show was so oversold they had to squeeze in extra tables and chairs, plus standing room. The first thing I did was look for a fire exit backstage. We were all backstage waiting to make our entrances, wondering how the audience would accept us over twenty years later. Would the magic still be there? The script called for the curtain to open on our empty set. When it did, we heard a burst of thunderous applause, and Jackie turned to me with a big grin and said, "We're home free."

It was amazing to see the busloads pull up to the hotel all day long to disgorge the gambling public. Sometimes it was difficult to maneuver through the lobby against the flow of incoming players. Jane Kean and I would be bundled up with sweaters and jackets against the November winds, looking more like Alice and Trixie than ourselves. To prove to you that fame is fleeting, Jane and I were attempting to move through the crowd one day when we were spotted. A very excited woman screeched, "Look! Look! There goes what's her name!"

And her friend yelled, "And that's the other one." What price glory?

I was called upon one more time by Philbin to help out. He asked me to meet him in one of the party rooms, where I found Jackie with his friend, and I guess mentor, Willie Mosconi (the greatest pool player in the known world, I'm told). They had obviously been playing for some time, doing trick shots. Jackie didn't know how to bring it to a close since he didn't want to offend Willie. My assignment was to watch for a little while and then break it up. Marilyn must have been taking a break, so I got the call. They were both great, and it was fascinating to watch, but I somehow cued an ending, and champ and challenger retired, each thinking the other guy had a fair stick that night.

Jackie and I stayed in touch throughout the years. My husband, Bob, and he got along famously, which proved they both had good taste. Bob and I were in Paris when Jackie was making *Gigot,* and we went to see him on the set. Jackie insisted we dismiss our car and drive back to the hotel in his Rolls-Royce. He was in great form and like a child in his enjoyment of the Rolls, but he was up to his old tricks. All three of us were smokers, and as I was smoking he suddenly yelled, "Look out, Aud, your ash dropped, and you've burned my rug!" For a moment I thought I had and almost fainted.

Then I saw the twinkle in his eye, examined the spot,

which was definitely an old burn, and said, "Oh, no. You don't get a new carpet out of me."

"But I gotcha again," said he, happily.

That was an especially good period for him in Paris. He loved the part he was playing.

A lovely touch about knowing Jackie was receiving either a wire or a phone call whenever he saw me in a performance, especially when I did a dramatic role. I did a two-hour Elmer Rice play, *The Grand Tour*, directed by Jack Smight, which was a tender story of an unmarried schoolteacher who had given up her life to care for aging parents. Upon their death, she takes her life savings to go on a grand tour of Europe, falls in love with a married man, gives him up, and in the last scene is back teaching school. After it aired, Jackie was on the phone to congratulate me and said I made him cry. The brash Broadway comic was a softy inside.

The years rolled on, and the thirty-nine shows we had filmed at DuMont were still running continuously in New York on WPIX. When they went off the air for a spell, there was such an outpouring of demand for their return that two enterprising young men, Peter Crescenti and Bob Columbe, started a fan club with the acronym RALPH, which stands for the Royal Association for the Longevity and Preservation of the Honeymooners.

In May of 1992, our ancient *Honeymooners* reruns were tying or topping Johnny Carson and leveling Arsenio Hall in the same time slot at WPIX. New Yorkers loved the Kramdens. Hey, we were neighbors, right? Through their loyal efforts, the thirty-nine *Honeymooners*es were put right back on the air and have been running ever since. The club grew to thousands of loyal fans, and the boys put on conventions once a year, which included contests for the best Alice, and the best Ralph or Norton, and the members arrived dressed as their favorite characters. They told me that at one convention, an elderly lady arrived in a very short skirt and apron, and when they asked her name to register her in the contest, she said, "I'm Alice Kramden at the age of ten."

They sold all kinds of memorabilia. Jackie gave them one of his bus driver's uniforms. Early in 1984, I received a call from a Rose Maione on my unlisted phone number. She wanted to know if they could buy any kind of souvenir I might have.

I said, "No, I can't sell you anything. But I will send you one of my housedresses and an apron I wore, if you like."

She was delighted, and I was curious. "How did you get my phone number?"

She stalled for a bit, then finally admitted she worked in a detective agency. Pretty good snooping.

The membership covered all ages and professions. There were doctors and lawyers, rock singers, all devoted fans. The boys also wrote books, which were very successful, as did another very talented lady, Donna McCrohan, with parts of scripts, trivia questions, and so on.

Jackie had sold all his rights to the thirty-nine filmed *Honeymooners* shows "much too early," according to his lawyer, Richard Green. Jackie didn't think so, though, since he didn't want to "be a film booker and stay in an office surrounded by numbers crunchers." He was an actor, a producer, a comedian, a composer. I guess he thought that was enough. Any more would interrupt his vast reading and pursuit of hypnotic powers.

So it was about thirty years after we filmed the thirty-nine shows that their success reminded Jackie that he had four years of "Honeymooners" shows in an air-conditioned vault in Miami. The first three years were the seasons of

1952–53, 1953–54, 1954–55 and the fifth year, 1956–57. According to his original contract with CBS, Jackie received a copy of every show. He made a deal with Viacom, and a press conference was called for February 6, 1985, at the "21" Club in New York. There were so many cameramen, they could have covered a war. All the networks and media were represented, and we were shuttled from room to room for interviews.

Jackie was in rare form and his usual ebullient self. In retrospect, I think he must have been bursting with pride at causing such a sensational reaction, but he was very humble and natural, taking it all in stride. Joyce and I had, inadvertently, showed up in the same color cocktail suit, almost matching Jackie's ever-present boutonniere.

Art and I did quite a few wraparounds to promote the so-called lost episodes. Doing a wraparound is appearing in between the film clips with anecdotes or descriptions of the clip to be shown. Jackie asked me to fly to Miami for the first one.

At his house, Marilyn and Jackie and I sat and watched a number of the old shows so he could select what he wanted to use. We laughed as if we were not watching ourselves. You see, we had never seen them. The shows were done live and went out over the air simultaneously. I had never seen what Jackie did at the end of each show when I would sit down in the chair and he would pace up and down behind me trying to apologize. I had to look straight out front while the audience screamed with laughter at his grimacing and gestures.

The next day we went to the studio to rehearse our dialogue and entrances and exits. They put up "The Honeymooners" set. We had a new crew, who had never worked with Jackie before, so they were completely unprepared for the speed with which he could dispatch an hour's show.

He'd direct, "I'll start in one" (that means alone in front of the curtain), "then Aud will come on stage left—I'll chat with her, run the clip. Next, open the curtain on the set, Aud will enter from the bedroom, do her dialogue, another clip," et cetera, et cetera, until he had laid out the whole show. We went through it once.

He told them where he wanted the monitors placed, ordered where he wanted the microphones hung in the audience to record their laughs, and started to walk out. Someone asked me where he was going. I said, "He's leaving."

The director nervously asked, "What time do you want tomorrow, Mr. Gleason? We have all day, and the audience will be in at 7:00 P.M."

Jackie turned to me and asked, "How long will it take you to get ready? Why don't we say 6:00 P.M.?" I agreed that would be fine and immediately sat down and started writing notes in my script.

The flustered director came over and said, "What are you doing?"

I said, "I'm writing down every move he gave me while I still remember them. I haven't worked with him in years, and I'm out of the habit. I suggest you do the same, because he will remember everything."

The crew was in a state of shock, but the next evening it went off as if we'd had it on the road for a year. Jackie was still Jackie!

The subsequent wraparounds were done in each of our homes and edited in later with the clips by a very unflappable producer, Andrew Solt.

The rest of 1985 was spent doing appearances for Showtime in San Francisco, Phoenix, and elsewhere, and picking up a collection of awards on the way.

What most authorized biographers don't seem to know is that our third season, 1954–55, we did "The Honeymooners" for the full hour. It was the idea of Leonard Stern, and all the writers came up with great scripts. When you see the reruns today and at the end of the half hour it says, "To be continued," you're watching one of our hour shows edited in half to fit the time slot.

On September 23, 1985, I was interviewed by Steve Edwards on his very popular Los Angeles show. I've always enjoyed his work, and I listen to him each day on ABC Radio. All these years I am always asked how I got the job with Jackie, and Steve Edwards was no exception. So I told him about being turned down, then having the pictures taken, and so on, and we had a very pleasant interview.

Oddly enough, a short time later, I was at home with the TV on, and there was Jackie being interviewed by Steve Edwards.

Edwards repeated what I had told him and asked, "Is that the way it really happened?"

I don't remember Jackie's exact words, but he answered to the effect that he certainly knew when someone was right for the part. But he said, "If that's the way Aud wants to remember it, it's all right with me."

I was stunned! He'd always loved telling how I got the part. Everyone on his staff knew the truth. The more I tried to figure it out, the more I began to think he was not the same confident man he used to be and, for some reason, the job selection story bothered his ego. He had been known to fudge on details before, but somehow I was disappointed to hear him deny the truth.

We all realized Jackie had changed in recent years. The

fun and joy seemed to have dribbled away from him. Maybe he was concerned about his health. It wasn't too long before he had his heart bypass, and his sensitivity and intuition may have nagged at his subconscious that time was running out. Who knows? I had never heard him complain. Whatever he felt, he kept to himself.

Old pals of mine working with Jackie had commented that a splendid professional had become difficult in every area—cantankerous, rude, overbearing to other actors. His drinking had also gone from a merry romp to a joyless ritual. It was making him a man he wouldn't have recognized, much less admired.

With me, he remained cheery, affectionate, optimistic. Still the deft performer, the charming companion. But there were too many reports of curious conduct from people who loved him. They were sad about the funny man.

When Jackie was inducted into the Television Academy Hall of Fame, he did not come to California to accept the honor himself. Instead, I was asked to accept it for him, which I was delighted to do. It was about time he received the homage due him.

We didn't dwell on the old days when we met and chatted. Indeed, Jackie was always interested in new plans, new events. "The past was either good or it was bad," he once told me. "Either way, you can't change it, so why live it over again? The only thing you can change is your future. Think about what's coming, not what went."

Jackie finally married Marilyn Taylor, the love of his life, and found he didn't have to stay up all night chasing around town to find happiness, since it was at home. That's not to say that he became a tabby cat, or lost his appreciation for fine spirits, but he managed to downshift gears without parking the car completely.

He had made some fine movies, playing dramatic parts in what was then daring countercasting. Now, he reversed his field and made some big box-office hits with Burt Reynolds, playing a wacko sheriff hot after smiling Burt, and later physical comedy with Richard Pryor. It wasn't art, but it was fast and funny and contributed to Jackie's very comfortable exchequer. He never did have to find that warehouse with a will call notice to retrieve the spare cash he'd wrapped up in his old socks.

In November 1990, I was on a flight to New York. It being a Monday, I asked the flight attendant for the newspaper *USA Today*. Monday's edition carries a top columnist I always read. To my great surprise, the column was about me, but it was all wrong, completely fictitious. The columnist quoted his source by name, a PR guy I couldn't recall who told him the most far-fetched, outrageous story about how I got the job. Since he wasn't there at the time, I couldn't imagine what prompted this delusion. I was so angry, I waited two weeks before making up my mind to call the columnist. In the interim, I called former colleagues to ask if any of them knew this tipster. The people who handled our publicity, and Jackie's, were Jack Goldstein of CBS and Lee Meyers. Lee was a top publicist who got us all the best magazine covers and stories, as well as Jack Goldstein. Hank Meyer was his main publicist in Miami, and a wonderful guy.

Determined to set the record straight, I called the columnist, who was very cooperative and friendly and said, "Well, if you write me the true story, I'll print it." I wrote the events down in detail and mailed it off. So far it has not appeared.

There was only one thing left to do, short of getting notarized statements from those who were involved. Track down the photographer! Bear in mind, this was thirty-nine years later, and I didn't know if he was still alive or had kept the pictures and negatives.

Going through an old address book in New York, I found his name and number. I made several calls, no answer. The last time I dialed, he answered. Wonderful Bill Mark, who had photographed everyone, had covered all the parties and events for years.

Crossing fingers, toes, and eyes, I posed my $64,000 question. "Bill, do you by any chance have the pictures you took of me in 1952 to get the job with Jackie?"

"Of course," he replied. "I never throw anything away."

Heaving a sigh of relief, I said, "I need them," and explained why.

He said, "I'll never forget that day." Bill, who had had no sleep the night before, even has a picture of himself sleeping while his assistant was developing the negatives and making the prints so we could deliver them that afternoon.

Next critical question. "When can I get them?"

He explained that he and his wife were moving to California and he had just sent a truckload of all his boxes of photos to the coast. He said he couldn't leave New York until they sold their apartment. We stayed in touch, and it was agonizingly long before they got a buyer. Months went by.

Eventually, I got a call. Bill said he was going through all the boxes looking for the pictures. As wonderful a photographer as Bill is, he would never get a prize for organization. Nothing was listed as to year or subject matter. He spent hours and days sifting through years of work, then called to say he had found them.

I was thrilled and invited him for lunch. Bill, being a dyed-in-the-wool New Yorker, said, "I'll come for lunch, but not at your house. I want to go to the Carnegie Deli." Joe Daley and I met him for lunch and took possession of the pictures as if they were platinum, and now you see them in this book. It just proves you should never throw anything away—phone numbers from the past, or boxes of photos, if you are a cameraman. God bless you, Bill.

Melancholy Serenade

He had been such an enthusiastic, optimistic individual that it was difficult to think of Jackie ever losing his great gusto for life. Yet serious illness saps the strength of giants, and in 1987 Jackie was waiting for the last act of cancer in a Florida hospital. All the medical devices were marshaled to make his passing not only painless but almost unnoticed, except for bleeps on the chart. Science could not save him, so it was better this way, he and his family were advised.

Jackie didn't see it the doctors' way. Exhausted from his battle with cancer, blurry from a pharmacy of drugs coursing through him, he whispered to his wife, Marilyn, "Get me home. If I'm going to go, it will be in my own bed, not in here, surrounded by strangers."

Responsible medical authority would not consider releasing a patient in Jackie's condition. So Marilyn stole her husband. She hired a private ambulance, led the attendants to Jackie's room, saw him placed on a gurney and taken downstairs. The hospital gurney wouldn't fit into the ambulance's patient compartment.

"Jackie," she explained to him, "the gurney won't fit. You'll have to stand up, so we can lift you into the ambulance."

He did, and they did, and he braved the trip home, sitting up, clutching his racking hurts and his wife's hand. He was obviously in pain, awesome pain, but he refused to let the agony win. He intended to die with dignity in his own house among those who loved him, with his wife and two beautiful daughters, Geraldine and Linda.

I had stayed in touch with both Marilyn and June Taylor. June had lost her husband after I lost Bob, and we had spent many a night on the phone crying with each other, sharing our heartbreak.

Marilyn and I decided that on a day Jackie was strong enough to speak to me on the phone, she would call me. When she did, she said she was in the closet with the phone because she wanted to tell me that Jackie's voice had diminished to a mumble that even she found unintelligible and maybe I would not be able to understand him too well. She left the closet, and I could hear her as she carried the phone over to the bed.

"It's Audrey," she said, then, thinking that in his condition the connection to my name might be vague, she corrected with "It's your Alice."

I greeted him but couldn't really understand what he mumbled at first.

So I said, "Jackie, I just called to tell you I love you, and it occurred to me that I never really thanked you for giving me the part of Alice."

Clear as crystal came his reply, "I knew what I was doing. I always knew what I was doing."

I said a few other predictable things about how all of us were praying for him, but I ended the call quickly so as not to overexert him. It had cost him untold energy to speak so clearly. The pride of the actor was still there.

As Marilyn took the phone away, I heard her say, "Oh great, you can speak clearly to Audrey, but you mumble to us," teasing him with a sweet voice.

She said she was astonished at his concentration and clarity, since he obviously knew Audrey was Alice and he was proud of his selection.

Several days later, on June 24, 1987, Jackie died in bed at home, with loved ones.

I was at home that evening and in the middle of a long phone call when the person whom I was talking to said, "Did you hear that Jackie Gleason died?"

Stunned, I said, "No, I haven't had the TV on, so I missed the news."

We hung up, and then my phone started ringing in earnest. A mobile crew was on the way to my house for an interview. I wasn't dressed or made up, so I rushed to get ready. Seems to me it was about nine o'clock. One crew after another arrived, so at 10:30, they were sending a limo for me to go to CBS first, then NBC in the San Fernando Valley, then ABC way downtown. At each network, phone calls were coming in from newspapers all over the country. It was about 2:00 A.M. when I got to NBC, and when I finished at ABC, the sun was coming up. The last interview I did was for WOR in the parking lot at ABC. Everyone wanted to hear recollections about this great star who had won the hearts of millions.

I flew to Miami June 26, getting there just in time for the

rosary. It was private, with just the people who really loved Jackie there. The next day, the funeral was very large and impressive. As we left St. Mary's Cathedral, fans were lined up on both sides of the street and even sitting on the roof-tops across the street.

June said, "Well, Jackie has his three favorite women here, his wife, his sister-in-law, and his stage wife."

In September, I was asked to do a tribute for Jackie at the Emmy Awards, where he had never received any recognition. I was delighted and assumed he would finally get an Emmy posthumously. I was wrong. The original idea was ill conceived—they wanted me to come onto "The Honeymooners" set as Alice on my way back from Ralph's funeral.

Aghast, I said, "Ralph Kramden didn't die, Jackie did."

The character of Ralph Kramden that Jackie had created, infused with mirth and madness, played with such bold yet endearing style, has become a defined character in American folklore. Ralph Kramden requires no requiem. He's as anxious, frustrated, lovable, and bombastic as he ever was.

Thank you for giving him to us, Jackie. . . .

So, as politically correct as I could be, I gently suggested that I would come up with a proper eulogy that I could deliver as myself, not Alice, in "The Honeymooners" set. I called my friend Harry Crane, who, you will remember, was one of Jackie's earliest writers on the old *Cavalcade of Stars* and was in on the birth of "The Honeymooners," and also with us at CBS. Harry is a very erudite man, as well as funny, great with words, and most important, he knew Jackie well.

Well, he wrote, and we worked together polishing the script. At this time, I had a bad back and was in a steel brace—I couldn't even get stockings on, much less high heels, but if Jackie could speak clearly to me, I could do this last thing for him. When you are dedicated to your role, you don't feel pain because your concentration is on your performance.

At rehearsal the day before the Emmy Awards, I was distressed to see the set all done in gray—even the kitchen table was a gray-brown. We always had a red-and-white or blue-and-white checked tablecloth on the kitchen table and usually dish towels hanging on the rack at the sink. Oh dear, I thought, how drab and somber; we need some color here. I asked them to please get a tablecloth and dish towels, which they assured me they would. That night, at home, I decided to take my own picnic tablecloth and towels, since I had a very strong feeling about what I would see the next day. Sure enough, they had a tablecloth. You guessed it . . . it was gray. So I replaced it with mine.

Jackie was not a gray man but a vibrant character of a thousand lights and colors.

I'm sure some of you feel that I've been too nice to Jackie in this recollection of five years on the carousel of early television, when we were making mistakes, making rules, and making quality entertainment all at the same time. He was the head and the heart of the whole circus. The fellow from Bushwick never looked over his shoulder to see if the rest of us were running to keep up. He made us all run faster, reach higher, go farther than we ever dreamed we could. It was a great and grand race, Jackie!

Well, this is my letter to him, and this is the way Jackie appeared to me—talented, buoyant, witty, smart, concerned, supportive, a dear friend

Audrey Meadows

To me, he was that rarity that women seem to see less and less—a gentle man.

> *And so good night, Ralph.*
> *I always said you were an angel,*
> *And I bet you are!*
>   *Your loving wife,*
>   *Alice*

Afterword . . .

Don't leave yet!

I've got a Curtain Speech!

It comes with the price of the book, and it is also something I have to get off my chest, or I'll have heartburn forever.

As I hope you realize by now, Jackie Gleason was one great comic actor, a one-man production company, and a gracious, charming, funny, funny fellow.

He was, of course, also a heavy drinker, a roisterer of the Old School, and a man who admired women as much as they did him.

Like that of Dean Martin, his thirsty and amorous life became part of the act. Jackie was never good at camouflage. And the audiences cheered his sporty asides concerning liquor, and high times, as part of the character and caricature of Broadway Jackie.

As I warned you early on, this essay wasn't a full-scale

biography of the man but a recollection of a bumptious, buoyant comic who made entertainment history and much enjoyed himself along the way.

Just about the time I got to the middle of this manuscript, two more Gleason biographies were published. Much like those I mentioned in Chapter One, one author liked Jackie as a person and a performer. The other, in the manner of revisionist historians who frown on all our heroes, scolded Jackie as not being up to the author's standards. He didn't challenge his talent, his achievement, his stature, but used words as hatchets to chop away at an entertainer whose only role in life was to entertain.

Recently, we've all been fed much sleaze and scandal by writers who reach deep into the mud to heave gobs at anyone who has stood tall enough to make a prime target.

I have no words of apology for Jackie. He wouldn't want any.

He was the complete performer.

The Great One shouldn't be recalled in tragic tones. He was a man of joy and laughter. He felt he owed his audience every spark of creativity, each nuance of technique, his mine of vitality, and his honest dedication to presenting the best of everything he could give to their entertainment.

That is what he did. Over and over. For all of his life.

"Take a final bow, Jackie. I can hear the house still applauding."